ORDER BOOKS - DIRECT

We're **faster** and **cheaper** than bookstores!
2 day delivery - **Satisfaction guaranteed!**

Please check <u>which</u> book you are ordering
and if you want 2 day Priority delivery.

Quantity	Book Title	Total Cost Per Book (Tax Included)		
		Reg. Mail	or	2 Day Priority
_____	**ATTENTION DEFICIT DISORDER** A Common but often over-looked disorder of Children ISBN 0-9619650-0-2	$11.95	or	$12.95
_____	**UNFULFILLED POTENTIAL** The ADD Child as an Adult ISBN 0-9619650-1-0	$11.95	or	$12.95

Send check or money order to:

FORRESST PUBLISHING
P.O. Box 155774
Fort Worth, TX 76155-0774

Watch for other books to be released by Mr. Hunsucker
in the summer of 1993 and spring of 1994.

NAME: _____ _

ADDRESS: _____ _

CITY: _____ S _ D1157893 _

(In Canada or outside the continental U.S.,
price will vary because of taxes and shipping.)

DEDICATION

I dedicate this to the people who have sent letters describing their situations, experiences, and how my book helped them.

I will always include some of your letters in my books because they give the research a <u>face</u>. Your letters help me address specific issues, which in turn, helps others.

They also keep me motivated and <u>focused</u>. In fact, my approach to work, and life in general, has been shaped by your letters.

Therefore, I thank <u>you</u> for helping <u>me</u>, help others.

Glenn Hunsucker

Unfulfilled Potential

by Glenn Hunsucker, M.A.

Forresst Publishing
P.O. Box 155774
Fort Worth, Texas 76155

ISBN 0-9619650-1-0

First Printing, 1993

CONTENTS

CHAPTER 1

AUTHOR'S NOTE
TO THE READER

I did not write this book for those who look at the world through "rose colored glasses". I wrote it for those who are willing to face reality.

I keep hearing people say that we need to stop focusing on the bad things that happen to those with untreated ADD.

They feel this is negative. They want to point out the ADD people who are successful. They believe this will give others hope.

I disagree. Focusing on those ADD people who are successful is the _most_ _negative_ thing you could possibly do. These people are _exceptions_ to the rule. You are ignoring the largest portion of ADD people when you do this. You are _ignoring_ the research. You are _ignoring_ reality.

Think about it! If we give the false impression that there are just as many successful ADD people as unsuccessful, we are sending the same message as those who don't believe that such a thing as ADD exists.

This message is the one that thousands of ADD children hear every day: You can do it, <u>if you just .... try .... a little harder</u>.

Once we get to this point, we end up repeating the same kind of thinking that has kept ADD from being understood or accepted for the last 50 years.

Here's how it progresses:

We point at an <u>exceptional case</u> (successful ADD person) and say: "See, they did it. If they can do it, you can do it."

This leads to the false conclusion that "effort", and not the disorder (ADD), is the problem.

The next typical conclusion, is that lack of <u>effort</u> is not the problem, laziness is the problem. From here, the next conclusion is that the child's laziness is not really the problem, the problem is the parents and their poor parenting skills ....and away we go. We are now back to square <u>one</u>. ADD once again fades into the background.

The purpose of my books, is to show people that ADD can cause severe problems <u>if</u> it isn't treated <u>properly</u>. <u>But</u>, if it <u>is</u> treated properly, these serious problems can be prevented. Therefore, I will say this: If <u>treated properly</u>, ADD adults can become just as successful as anyone else.

I wrote this book about the ADD adults who have had to struggle.

Some people with ADD will not have severe problems. I'm not concerned with them at this point. I care that they have problems, but I feel the focus should first be on those with more serious problems.

Because ADD has been overlooked for so long, there is much to be done. Unfortunately, this means that some areas will have to be overlooked until the professionals, and society at large, gain a better understanding of ADD. Once a basic understanding of ADD is developed by the general public, then will be the time to focus on other areas.

There will be other people who write about ADD and they will focus on the "superficial" aspects of the disorder. This is not to say that people won't receive help from these books. I'm sure that some will. However, they do not provide the in-depth understanding of ADD that is needed at this time in history. People need to be told about ADD in a straight-forward and blunt manner. This is what I try to do.

This is not a novel. This is a book about a serious disorder that has caused serious problems. Therefore, you need to understand that what you are about to read, was not written for its entertainment value, or as an attempt to create a perfectly written piece of literature for the experts. It was written to communicate information.

CHAPTER 2

INTRODUCTION TO ATTENTION DEFICIT DISORDER

ADD is an extremely serious disorder. It is much more than a learning problem that effects schoolwork. Research indicates that those who have had ADD have a higher probability of becoming involved in alcohol or drugs, dropping out of school and becoming involved in illegal activities.

In my first book I made some strong statements regarding how important this disorder is to society. Since that time, I not only reaffirm my statements, I am willing to make them even stronger. My statements were, that ADD is a prime cause of the following three problems:

- Crime rate

- Dropout rate

- Alcohol and drug abuse

I not only restate this, but I am now willing to confidently state that ADD accounts for 30% to 40% of the people in these three categories. The evidence and research is out there to support my statements. I am not the only one who believes that ADD has a strong impact on our society. However, I will say that I am one of the few willing to risk the criticism that comes with making such claims. Only history will prove if I was crazy or ahead of the times.

It doesn't matter whether or not I receive credit for bringing ADD to the forefront, but I feel it's time for someone to get bold and speak to these issues. The other "experts" seem to be more concerned about what their colleagues will think, so they play it safe and discuss ADD in superficial terms. As far as I'm concerned, the only thing that really matters is that the children, and adults who have the disorder, get treated properly. This may allow them to live a normal life. Hopefully, this book will help them achieve that goal.

In order to give you a perspective on ADD, consider the following. Research indicates that ADD is from 3% to 10% of the average population. "Average population" means that if you selected people at random, between 3% to 10% of them would have ADD. That means, out of 100 people that you pick, between 3 and 10 will have ADD.

Now, let us consider special populations. In other words, a special population is no longer a random sample of people walking the streets. A special population is people with certain problems or certain skills. (The percentage of people who have ADD, increases or decreases in special populations.)

Let us first consider the population of those who had no serious academic, behavior or emotional problems, and became extremely successful in business. You will not find a large number of people with ADD in this group. You will find <u>less</u> than the average of 3% to 10 %. I estimate that less than 1% of those in this special population have ADD.

The next special population to consider is those with learning disabilities. Research indicates that ADD exists in 60% to 80% of this group. Remember, the average population only has 3% to 10%. We are no longer dealing with the average population. We are dealing with the special population of those with learning disabilities.

The next special population is drop outs. There are no exact figures, but research does indicate that ADD is higher among drop outs. I estimate that the percentage of drop outs with ADD is 30% to 40%. Again, the average population is 3% to 10% but we are not dealing with the average population.

Another population to consider is those who abuse alcohol or drugs. Research indicates that those ADD adults who have not been treated, have a high probability of becoming involved in alcohol or drug abuse. I estimate that 30% to 40% of those who abuse alcohol and drugs have ADD. Again, we are not dealing with the average population.

The next special population is those involved in crime. I would estimate that 30% to 40% of this population have undiagnosed and untreated ADD. That means, if you gather the criminals and test all of them, I would estimate that 30% to 40% have ADD. (Perhaps even more.)

As you can see, I feel that the three specific

problem areas that are of most concern to us in the United States are directly affected by ADD. Why is it that no one pays attention to ADD? To explain this is difficult. I am writing another book to address this. This topic was going to be a chapter, but as I wrote it, I recognized that it was impossible to address all of the relevant issues in just a chapter. I also recognized that this information was extremely important to us as a society. Therefore, it warranted a thorough inspection.

I say that if we want to reduce the crime, alcohol/drug abuse and dropout rate, ADD should be the starting place. Obviously, not everyone who is an alcoholic, drug abuser, criminal or a dropout has ADD. However, we could make a big dent in these areas if we focused upon ADD and properly treated these individuals early.

CHAPTER 3

DESCRIPTION OF ADD

This book is about ADD in adults. However, I must first explain the disorder in children in order for the reader to see how the accumulative effect of ADD impacts a person's later years. For more information on children, please read my first book.

Before I explain the symptoms of this disorder, I must first give you some background information.

Although many of you may not be familiar with the term Attention Deficit Disorder (ADD), you are probably familiar with the term hyperactivity. Hyperactivity used to be the term used for children who are now diagnosed as ADD. Other terms that were used before hyperactivity were minimal brain damage, hyperkinesis, and the broad label of learning disabled. You may wonder why the name was changed. It may seem that the name was changed in order to be more stylish. Actually, the reason for the change is logical, and beneficial to the many people who may otherwise be overlooked when other terms are used.

Through research, it was discovered there were a

number of children who exhibited the same problems that hyperactive children exhibited but, they were not overly active. In other words, they had short attention spans, had difficulty concentrating, and difficulty with school work, but they did not bounce off the wall. Therefore, the diagnostic category of hyperactivity did not fit these children. These children were overlooked. Consequently, it was discovered that the major problem with these children, including the hyperactive ones, was their attention. Hence, the name Attention Deficit Disorder was used to include both the hyperactive and non-hyperactive children.

Under this broad category of Attention Deficit Disorder, three levels were identified. ADD with hyperactivity, ADD without hyperactivity, and ADD residual type. (I have developed 12 categories of ADD that go well beyond these 3 levels. This book will be released in August of 1993.)

As previously mentioned, the major difficulty of children with ADD is attentional. Forget about hyperactivity. Activity level has very little to do with this disorder.

Here is a list of problems that are related to school:

- They have difficulty maintaining attention in the classroom as well as at home.

- They are impulsive and have difficulty sticking with tasks for long periods of time.

- They are disorganized and do not complete their work at school or home.

- Their school work is usually sloppy and inaccurate.

- These children may be seen as not listening to what they have been told.

- They sometimes seem to lack common sense and overlook the obvious.

As you read these traits, remember that these children grow up to be adults. That means these traits may either change or be modified through the years. In some cases, the adult may continue to have the exact same problems they had as children.

These children usually have more problems in a group situation than when they are one on one. The reason that group situations seem to be difficult for these children is because they are easily distracted both visually and auditorily.

Here is a list of problems related to their behavior:

- Parents may have a difficult time getting the child to obey or to follow through on directives.

- The parent may discover that these children may have trouble sticking to one play activity for any period of time.

- These children are prone to have temper outbursts and unpredictable behaviors.

- Parents sometimes worry that these children have no conscience.

- They may have difficulty keeping friends because they usually play rougher than the average child.

- The overly active children may appear to have never ending energy.

- It is sometimes hard to get them to take a nap, and they appear to need less sleep than most children.

At this point I must state that <u>all</u> children exhibit the traits previously mentioned. However, the difference between the average child and an ADD child is one of degree. They do these things <u>more often</u> than the average child.

To confuse you more, I will state that this disorder is not exactly the same in every child. For example, one child may have learning problems to a severe degree, while another child may not exhibit such obvious learning problems. One child may exhibit these problems at the age of three or four years, while another child may not exhibit school difficulties until the seventh or eighth grade. Because the symptoms differ from child to child, diagnosing ADD is sometimes difficult.

ADD is a common disorder. This is an important piece of information. I am not writing about a disorder that occurs less often than other problems. Research shows that between three to five percent of children have this disorder. Some estimates go as high as ten percent.

Although ADD children have problems and are impulsive, they are not necessarily less intelligent. In fact, many have an extremely high level of intelligence and are rather creative. These children appear to do poorly in the classroom, not because of a lack of intelligence, but because of their short term memory, short attention span, and distractibility. This makes it hard for them to concentrate and complete tasks.

Many of these children have been found to have poor social development. Again, not all children, just some. These children, especially the ones with hyperactivity, are often behavior problems.

ADD children without hyperactivity may be totally opposite . . . . they may be quiet, guilt ridden, down on themselves, or give their toys away. They will not try to push themselves into situations with other people and many times they may be seen as a nerd, shy, or withdrawn. Therefore, it is not easy to pinpoint a child with ADD just based on their social functioning. As I mentioned earlier, one child may manifest symptoms of the disorder in one manner while another may manifest symptoms in an opposite manner.

This disorder is ten times more common in boys than in girls. It also appears to be more common among the 1st born. The disorder is also hereditary. This means that there is likely to be a history of academic or behavior problems in the family. Drug usage (alcohol) is also common in the family history.

Some of these children may exhibit a low tolerance for frustration and have mood swings. They sometimes develop low self-esteem and the school drop out rates among youngsters with ADD is very high. Research also indicates that teenagers with ADD are more likely to become involved in Juvenile crime.

The disorder does not disappear at puberty. Some symptoms, such as excessive over-activity, may disappear but attention problems remain.

The following is a list of symptoms common to ADD children with hyperactivity.

- They have trouble concentrating on things for a long period of time.

- They become easily distracted (visually/auditorily).

- They have trouble following directions.

- They do not finish what they start.

- They act before they think.

- They need more supervision than other children.

- They are usually disruptive in class.

- They do not like to wait their turn in games.

- They go from one activity to another and have trouble sticking to one thing.

- Signs of the disorder are evident before age 7.

- Loses things (i.e., school work, books, etc.).

- Answers questions before they are completed.

- Squirms or fidgets (teenagers may feel restless).

- Engages in risk-taking behavior.

- Intrudes on conversations.

- Trouble following through on directions.

- May talk excessively.

- Overall disorganization or extremely organized.

ADD children without hyperactivity exhibit the following symptoms:

- They have trouble concentrating on things for a long period of time.

- Easily distracted.

- They have trouble following directions.

- They do not finish what they start (although they may try harder than those who are hyperactive).

- They lose things (i.e., school work, books, etc.).

- Overall disorganization or overly organized.

- Seem to be depressed and daydream a great deal.

- May be meek and not speak out in defense of themselves as their hyperactive counterparts might.

In adulthood, many of these symptoms may remain, but most of the time, they have been modified to some degree.

CHAPTER 4

CAUSE OF ADD

I'm not going to get into a long discussion about possible causes of ADD. I am only going to mention heredity. ADD Is hereditary. This is the source.

In future books, I will focus on this area in more detail. However, in this book, I will be brief and incomplete.

There is always the possibility of future changes. Therefore, I will not claim that ADD is <u>absolutely, positively, 100%</u> hereditary. But, for the last 20 years, the evidence has been strongly in favor of this.

Instead of using the word <u>cause</u>, I will use the word <u>source</u>. Heredity is the <u>source</u> of ADD.

I'm currently investigating and compiling information on physical problems of ADD Adults and Children. I hope to find something helpful. This has been done before, but it seems that those who have done it, were <u>biased</u> at the outset. They often worked for a special interest group (an example of this is Allergists or Drug Companies. We know what they were looking for).

I know that I will be more objective than others because I <u>don't</u> have a <u>vested</u> interest in any particular group. I'm not doing this for Doctors, Allergists, Hospitals, Psychologists, Drug Companies, or Nutritionists. I'm doing this for the people who have ADD.

<u>Attention Deficit Disorder</u>, with or without hyperactivity, is a <u>neurological</u> problem. It does not occur in the muscles, arms or legs. It occurs in the brain. It is known that this disorder is a chemical imbalance. It is <u>not</u> a psychological problem. It has also been shown that <u>medication is the only</u> effective <u>treatment.</u>

Studies have been done on twins that point to the conclusion that the disorder is genetic. Research indicates that there is usually a history of alcoholism, illegal behavior, and depression among family members of ADD children.

Unfortunately, when the aforementioned <u>traits of the family</u> are listed (i.e., alcoholism, depression), most people are apt to see these as the cause. These <u>are not the cause.</u> They may have had an effect on the person, but they did <u>not cause</u> ADD.

Heredity explains the source of ADD but does not explain how it occurred in the first individual in the family. This is a mystery that may never be solved. Some people report that they see no hereditary link. Therefore, they assume that ADD must not be the problem.

Remember, ADD doesn't <u>have</u> to be present in other family members. The main point is this: I do <u>not</u>

diagnose ADD with this information anyway. It really doesn't matter if there is a link. I gather this information, but it's only a small, small part of my evaluation process.

Researchers believe that the major difficulty in the ADD brain is with the neurotransmitter. I am not a scientist or a medical doctor, but I will try to relate to you in terms that I understand, what this means.

The brain has millions of neurons. Between these neurons is a chemical called a neurotransmitter. This chemical relays messages of pain, memory, and other human actions. Scientists feel that the major problem is this chemical. Hence, a chemical imbalance. The only way that the chemical can be balanced is by the introduction of another chemical. This means medication. Research has become so exact that they feel they have located the part of the brain that is the major problem.

This appears to be the pre-frontal cortex. It is responsible for planning and regulating complex behaviors such as anticipating and preparing for future events. Researchers have noted that people who have had head injuries, sometimes have symptoms that are similar to ADD. They are inattentive, distractible, impulsive, and unable to follow rules (This is not ADD. This is brain damage).

Two people can have ADD but be very different. I will try to help you understand how people with the same disorder (ADD) can have opposite symptoms.

Remember, ADD is a chemical imbalance. This means that the chemical between the neurons, which is responsible for "relaying information", does not relay the proper message. In other words, it gives the wrong signal to the brain.

For example: most people with ADD have an unusual pain tolerance. I say unusual, because some have a very high pain tolerance and some have a very low pain tolerance. This occurs because the chemical between the neurons relays the wrong information. It relays a message that allows one person to feel very little pain and another to feel too much.

Other examples of extremes are: some crave sugar and others eat very little; Some are very outgoing and hyper, while others are quiet and shy; Some make decisions very quickly while others take too long.

All of these "extreme opposites" are due to the "messages" that are relayed by a chemical imbalance.

Why does one person receive one message and another person receives another? I don't know. This is one of the things that may never be known.

Many people have trouble believing that a chemical imbalance can cause so many problems. My response to this, is to ask these people to think of other things they believe to be true. For example: psychological principles such as multiple personalities are accepted rather easily by society. Believing someone can have 10 or 11 different personalities seems harder to believe than a chemical imbalance. Also, Einstein's theory, as well as those of recent scientists, seem harder to believe than a chemical imbalance.

To go one step further, believing in God is more complex than a chemical imbalance. Some people believe in astrology. Is this _easier_ to believe than a chemical imbalance? Allergies _don't cause_ ADD, but if you are willing to believe allergies have an effect on the way a person feels, is this harder to believe than the chemical imbalance I described earlier?

To me; it's pretty simple. ADD is a chemical imbalance in the brain that is inherited. This chemical merely relays the wrong "message", which causes a variety of problems for the person who happens to have it. I see nothing mystical about this.

WHAT DOESN'T CAUSE ADD

Sugar and Food Additives

Nutritionists swear that food additives and refined sugars cause ADD. It is obvious that sugar does cause unusual reactions in some people. However, it is not the _cause_ of ADD. Reducing a person's intake of sugar will not cure ADD. Remember, the treatment has to be directed at the cause. Sugar and food additives do not cause ADD. Therefore treating these will not cure it.

Don't get me wrong. I have no doubt that _what we eat_ has a _great deal to do_ with _how we feel_, both physically and emotionally.

Body builders are the best proof of how important diets can be. Their muscles are built from what they eat, or put into their body. Lifting weights break down the muscles; what they eat, builds them up.

Therefore, don't assume that I'm suggesting that diets, vitamins or sugar don't have an effect on a person. They absolutely _do_. However, people who read this book need to understand that this book is about <u>one</u> particular disorder, and not a book on the overall benefits of diet and nutrition.

The <u>confusion</u> about nutrition, sugar, diets, and ADD is often caused by books written by <u>nutrition</u> experts. They know a great deal about nutrition and the effects it has on the body. What they <u>don't know</u> a great deal about, is <u>ADD</u>.

I personally listen to what nutritionists say about certain foods, because they have spent a great deal of time studying this. I have spent a great deal of time studying ADD and therefore, <u>they</u> should pay attention to what <u>I</u> say about ADD.

Nutrition is not the solution to the world's problems and neither is ADD. We need to be cautious when making claims. This is why I use percentages when discussing the number of people who may have ADD in certain populations. I don't want people to think that ADD causes everything. I hope nutritionists will do the same.

I think it's important to point out the connection between ADD and sugar or dietary changes. The connection is, that <u>those with ADD metabolize</u> sugar <u>differently</u> than others.

Many people think that sugar <u>causes</u> ADD. <u>It does not cause ADD.</u> As a matter of act, sometimes it's just the opposite. ADD causes an <u>unusual</u> need for sugar. ADD is a chemical imbalance that causes a person to need more <u>or</u> less of a particular nutrient.

Because of the hundreds of ADD people with whom

I've worked, I've seen ADD children who ate very few sweets. As a matter of fact, they didn't like desserts or candy. Most people never hear of these ADD children.

Ironically, after treatment with medication, the people with unusual appetites often start eating foods in a more normal fashion. Those who crave sweets no longer crave them. Those who eat very few sweets may consume more.

Again, I believe in watching one's diet and taking vitamins. However, we must not get brainwashed into thinking that vitamins and other "natural" substances will solve all problems. Even medication, the most effective treatment, sometimes doesn't solve all problems. However, it solves more problems, more often, faster, and for a longer period of time than anything else. It's unlikely that this will change anytime soon.

Allergies

Allergies may produce some symptoms that are similar to ADD. This is not unusual. However, these are merely overlapping symptoms and not ADD. Those with ADD often have allergies. Research shows that these are associated problems that often occur in those with ADD. Why? No one knows.

Very simply, if someone is treated for allergies and the symptoms of "ADD" (or what is thought to be ADD) disappear, then they had allergies. They did not have ADD (ADD consists of more than the 1 or 2 symptoms allergists call ADD).

Fetal Alcohol Syndrome (FAS)

This is the latest attempt at "re-inventing" the wheel. FAS is due to the mother drinking when she was pregnant. I don't doubt that FAS exists, just as allergies and brain damage. However, people are mis-interpreting the data on FAS.

Research on the affects of FAS has been directed at adopted children who have behavioral or academic problems. They found that the mothers drank during pregnancy and blame this drinking for the child's problems.

It's extremely important to note that ADD occurs 4 times more often in adopted children as in the general population. Remember, ADD is hereditary. For a quick summary of the hereditary link between ADD and adopted children, please note the following:

One parent has ADD.
↓
Therefore, they are impulsive, have a strong sex drive and low self-esteem due to failures at home, school and with peers.
↓
They are also more prone to drug or alcohol use (or abuse).
↓
Due to traits of ADD, they become pregnant or get someone pregnant due to not considering the consequences of their actions.
↓
They drink during pregnancy.
↓
They are young and irresponsible and unable to take care of a child.
↓

They give up the child for adoption.

↓

The Adoption Agency doesn't gather the needed background information on the natural relatives. (ADD may have existed in other family members, but there is no evidence)

↓

At age 5 or 6, the child starts having academic, behavioral, or emotional problems.

↓

A researcher looks for a common link between adopted children who have <u>problems</u>.

↓

There is insufficient information on the family background (hereditary factors).

↓

Therefore, the researcher can only go back as far as when the mother was pregnant.

↓

Of the adopted children used in the research, the mothers consuming alcohol during pregnancy was the only common link.

↓

Therefore, he concludes this is the reason for the child having academic, behavioral, or emotional problems.

↓

He now <u>re-invents</u> the wheel.

This is one of many reasons ADD never gets the high profile it should.

[As a rule of thumb, remember the following:]

- Someone has a head injury that causes them to have symptoms similar to ADD. This is <u>Brain Damage</u>, not ADD.

- Someone has allergies that cause symptoms similar to ADD. These are <u>allergies</u>, not <u>ADD</u>.

- Someone eats chocolate or a great deal of sweets that cause symptoms similar to ADD. This is a <u>reaction</u> to chocolate or sugar. This is <u>not</u> ADD.

- ADD is <u>hereditary</u>. This is the <u>source</u>.

Letter # 1

Dear Mr. Hunsucker,

Thank you so much for your book ADD. I don't think there could be a parent who could remain dry-eyed who has a child who has ADD after reading your book. You see, my son who is 12 has ADD. I was a nurse for 20 years - 3 years in pediatrics - and he was not diagnosed until age 9 when I found a friend's child had similar symptoms - It is so little spoken of.

He was treated for 2 years on medication with dramatic results in improvement, but since reaching puberty it is no longer effective. Today, we are trying another medication and I pray that it will work.

He's such an intuitive child and has such insight into his illness. He asked the doctor today, "if this doesn't work, will you give UP?", his eyes pleading and helpless. I'm not sure where to turn next if it doesn't work, but he doesn't know this. His grades are F, F, B, FFF, A-, FF. Daily he's on a roller coaster.

His Uncle (Father's Brother) I believe has ADD. He turned to alcohol at age 12 and is now in jail for suspected murder. He is now 35 and had problems as a school dropout, alcohol, drugs, not holding jobs, leaving his wife and daughter, etc. I know that ADD is hereditary.

Another reason I feel it is down-played is because of parental pride. We all want to have the "perfect" child. Especially in upper-middle class families such as ourselves. We feel if we just try harder or if they will try harder, we can do it alone. Well, we can't!

Thank you for taking time to read my letter and for your validating many issues that I know to be true in your book.

Sincerely,

Diedre

AUTHOR'S RESPONSE

Note that she was a nurse for 20 years and from the upper-middle class. This is important to know because she still didn't know anything about ADD until her son was 9 years old.

My point is: if someone this educated has a child with ADD but still overlooks it, what happens to those children who have less educated parents who are in the lower socio-economic group? I say, even more of these children and adults are over-looked, especially among minorities.

She notes that he was treated successfully until he reached 11 or 12 years of age (puberty). As I stated in the treatment portion of this book, puberty is the age in which the type of medication may need to be changed. What she is experiencing is what a lot of parents experience when their ADD child reaches this age.

Letter #2

Dear Mr. Hunsucker,

I bought one of your books about 9 months ago and I was very pleased with it. I have one child that will be 9 years old in June and she was diagnosed as being ADD about 3 years ago. She has had a lot of trouble because last year they had labeled her a troublemaker in school. She has been suspended from school twice this year.

I also have a son that will be 12 in November. He has been diagnosed as having ADD and dyslexia. The doctor has them both on medicine. I don't know how I could make it with out them being on the medication.

You are right about people not understanding this disorder. I myself had a lot of problems in school and dropped out at the 11th grade and its been real hard for me to hold a job for more than a year or so. I have 5 brothers and 1 sister, and I believe 3 of them have it besides myself. One of my brothers dropped out of school when he was 15 and in the last 10 years, he has had about 10 different jobs. He is also an alcoholic and sometimes takes a lot of drugs. All of my brothers and my sister dropped out except the youngest brother. I do believe it comes from my mother; she dropped out of school in the 8th grade.

There are a lot of times I cry and cry, and wish that I hadn't had any children because I see how hard it is for them, but then I say we learn so much more about them each year, maybe by the time my children have children, they will know more and can treat it better.

Respectfully yours,

Sue

AUTHOR'S RESPONSE

What can I add to this?

If you, the reader, don't get the point, then read it again.

CHAPTER 5

TREATMENT

First, let me say that there are thousands of treatment methods for ADD. There are thousands of treatment methods for headaches also.

Think about what I just said.

The word treatment, when used without an adjective, means nothing. The adjective of which I speak is . . . <u>effective</u>.

Professionals constantly talk of treatment methods but don't separate the effective from the ineffective.

If you think about it, anything can be considered "treatment". You can "treat" ADD by carrying a rock in your left pocket. This is not effective treatment, but it's treatment.

Therefore, I'm going to talk about the most effective treatment for ADD.

The <u>only</u> treatment found to be effective is medication.

As stated in the "cause" section of this book, ADD is a physiological problem. It is a neurotransmitter chemical imbalance.

Remember, I'm talking about ADD and <u>all</u> of the symptoms that come along with it. (Not just excessive activity.)

Proper treatment of ADD with medication is essential. Remember ... <u>proper</u> treatment.

The reason I emphasize <u>proper</u> is because this can make the difference between success and failure. The type of medication, time of day, dosage and increasing at the proper time, are all important.

If <u>one</u> of these is done improperly, it can sabotage treatment. Since ADD is not well understood, even those who are diagnosed as having ADD, are not assured of being properly treated.

I was never interested in becoming as familiar with medication as I have. I was afraid that people would think that I was trying to "pan" myself off as a Medical Doctor. Therefore, I was hesitant to talk about dosage, time of day, or types of medication. The last thing I wanted to do was challenge a Medical Doctor. However, after seeing numerous individuals receive the improper treatment, I felt that I had to become more active and assertive in the medical treatment. Because Doctors were improperly treating ADD, some clients were not receiving the help they needed.

Because of this lack of success, these people started doubting ADD and whether or not it existed. It also cast doubt upon my credibility. Needless to say, I felt

I had to do something to get these people the help they needed, as well as to protect the credibility of ADD and myself.

The reason I'm going through such a long explanation at this time, is because I will give some specific information about the treatment with medication.

Since I'm not a Medical Doctor, I felt you needed an explanation as to why I was giving this information. A more detailed chapter on treatment is presented in my first book and I will write an even more thorough book on treatment at a later date. I could not fit all of the information into this book. I just wanted to say a few things about treatment near the front of this book, because it is often mentioned in the first few chapters.

I felt the reader needed to understand a <u>few</u> things about treatment before reading other chapters. However, I didn't want to go into detail this early in the book because it would "slow you down".

The main topic of this book is ADD in adults, so I wanted the reader to get to the chapters that might be of more interest to them than treatment at this point in time.

Most Common Medications

NAME	BEGINNING DOSE	AVERAGE DOSE
Methylphenidate (Ritalin)	5-10 mg <u>before</u> meals. Gradual increases of 5-10 mg/week.	10 mg - 3 to 4 times per day.
D-Amphetamine (Dexedrine)	5 mg/week until proper level.	3 to 4 times per day.
Pemoline Cylert)	37.5 mg. Increase 18.75 weekly until proper dose.	75 - 150 mg. per day.

Other Medications

Imipramine (Tofranil) or Desipramine (Norpramin)	25 mg. Increase by 25 mg. weekly until proper dose.	75 - 150 mg. per day. All at once or split into 2 doses.

Reasons to Seek Treatment:

If a person needs a reason to seek treatment, here are a few:

1. To improve job performance
2. To improve family life
3. To improve ability to learn
4. To improve the ability to handle finances responsibly
5. To improve overall feelings of confidence
6. To decrease the degree of mood changes
7. To prevent serious car accidents
8. To prevent suicidal thoughts
9. To prevent being sent to prison
10. To prevent death
11. To prevent alcohol/drug abuse

As stated elsewhere in this book, I can't predict the future. Therefore, I can't say that the aforementioned will happen to anyone who goes untreated. However, these are some of the problems that untreated ADD causes. If ADD is treated, the chances of these things occurring is reduced.

CHAPTER 6

TRAITS OF ADD ADULTS

The following traits of ADD adults were discovered through the research of others:

- **More unsuccessful (in work)**

- **More unhappy**

- **More inattentive**

- **Less honest**

- **Lower self-esteem**

- **More nervous**

- **More careless**

- **Poor relationships**

Let us remember that everyone is different, even those who have ADD. Therefore, do not assume that the above traits apply to everyone who has ADD. Some may apply and others may not. The "degree" of each trait may vary also. These traits closely resemble those of children with ADD. The difference is, that the adults have endured more years of frustration. This is an important point. The accumulative effect of this frustration can't be accurately measured.

Here is a brief description of each trait:

More unsuccessful

This relates to their inability to stick to a task for an extended period of time. As we know, to become successful in any field, we must be able to keep going even when we become frustrated with the task. Those with ADD usually have a low frustration tolerance. Therefore, they may give up earlier than they should. They get close to success, but quit too soon. Some ADD adults may be workaholics, but still remain unsuccessful. This is because they have to spend more time at their job to keep up with the work others do in eight hours.

Because they have trouble working for others, they may gravitate towards being their own boss. This may help them avoid dealing with authority figures and allow them to structure their time. However, when you own your own business, paperwork is a necessary evil. This may cause them problems.

More unhappy

Several factors account for this. One is the fact that they have had ADD all their life and have had to struggle harder than the average person. The stress of just living has taken an accumulative toll. They have had little success in school (as children) and they have had problems with parents. As stated previously, they may also have struggled in their jobs for a number of years. They have never been able to fulfill their potential. When all of these experiences are combined, it is easy to see why they are unhappy.

Now, another aspect of being unhappy is physiological. Remember, people with ADD have strong emotions due to a chemical imbalance (ADD). When they feel depressed, they feel it more severely than the average person. If the depression is "triggered" by the experiences previously mentioned, they may feel more depressed than others who have had similar experiences.

Depression (due to a chemical imbalance) is often present in those with ADD. Therefore, a traumatic event may not be necessary for them to become depressed. It just occurs. Exactly why, no one knows. It's the same thing that happens with ADD children. They may do well one day but horribly the next. Again, no one knows why. For some reason, the chemical is causing more problems that particular day.

More inattentive

Again, trouble paying attention continues to be a problem for ADD adults. This is also the most common trait among ADD children. The difference now is that inattentiveness relates to areas other than schoolwork. ADD adults are not only inattentive in academic endeavors but also in their work and personal relationships. In the area of work, their inattentiveness to detail may result in poor job performance. As a spouse, they may not "pick up on" the problems in their marriage or with their children. They have problems with long discussions because they can't sustain their attention for a long period of time. They may also jump from topic to topic, which means that an argument may never be completed. Because ADD adults are prone to have bad tempers, they may blow up and get angry because of becoming frustrated with a discussion.

ADD adults are intelligent and can <u>tell you</u> what they should or shouldn't be attentive to. Their problem lies in their actual ability to do it.

Less honest

Again, not all ADD adults are less honest than others. A large number are. This is not necessarily due to them being deliberately dishonest. They may have a different standard than that of others. Therefore, <u>withholding</u> information is not seen as being dishonest, but as a method of accomplishing what they want.

They don't stick to strict rules for doing things. Again, the type of rules they break vary in degree. For example: if the ADD adult works in an office setting and employees are not supposed to wear short-sleeve shirts, the ADD adult is more likely to break this rule than others. A more extreme example is the ADD adult who actually breaks the law by stealing from others.

Lower self-esteem

It doesn't take much explanation to see why ADD adults have a lower self-esteem than others. Self-esteem is developed by having successes and being able to praise yourself for these successes. Since the ADD adult has not experienced a large number of successes, they have not been able to praise themselves for their accomplishments. In fact, they are more prone to give themselves negative messages.

More nervous

This relates to their restlessness and constant feeling of wanting to keep busy. They may not be "hyperactive" in motor activity, but their thoughts and ideas may be in constant motion.

More careless

This trait is directly a result of their inability to sustain concentration and pay attention to details. This kind of problem will cause them to lose jobs.

An important finding related to carelessness is that ADD adults have more car accidents than the average person. No doubt this is due to not paying attention to what they are doing. I've had numerous parents report that before treatment, their son's driving scared them. After treatment, the improvement in driving was amazing. Their child would now concentrate on what he was doing and not be in such a rush.

Poor relationships

I put this near the end because it is more of a result of the previously-mentioned traits. Hopefully, you can see how a person who is inattentive to the feelings of others will have difficult relationships. Because they are less happy, have bad tempers, change jobs often, make careless mistakes, have low self-esteem and lack of confidence, their personal relationships may not last. Not many people want to be around a person like this for a long period of time.

ADD adults are very good at <u>starting</u> relationships. They often give a very good <u>first</u> impression. This ability allows them to be good at manipulating others. Outsiders see them much differently than those who know the ADD adult well. Therefore, they may have trouble believing the negative comments about the ADD adult (parents of ADD children experience this often).

Other Problems

The following list is based on my experience:

- Interrupts others
- Difficulty dealing with paper work
- Disorganized life-style
- Takes on too many projects
- Low stress tolerance
- Is seen as untrustworthy

Interrupts others

When an ADD adult wants to make a comment, they usually make it as soon as possible. If they don't, they will forget it. They have an intense emotional feeling that makes it difficult for them to control themselves. Needless to say, they often interrupt the person who is talking.

I have presented seminars and workshops on ADD in which ADD adults (some untreated) were in attendance. They would interrupt or "blurt out" comments that obviously annoyed other people at the workshop. Eventually, others would laugh or just look at them and roll their eyes.

When I observed this, I took it as an opportunity to give an "object lesson." I explained to this person that I wasn't trying to embarrass them, but that it was a rare moment for everyone in the room because we could discuss one particular ADD trait from several perspectives.

I then explained why they interrupted, and how others interpreted this. They interrupted, or finished my sentences, because they became excited about what I am saying. Either they had thought the same thing, or had the same experience, and just couldn't control their emotions. They were not aware of how others viewed their actions. They were also not aware that others were laughing at them, even when their comments indicated intelligence and insight. Their actions caused others to ignore the message.

This short conversation changed the "mood" of the meeting. The person who interrupted, worked hard to avoid interrupting and the rest of the group no longer glanced at each other. They now viewed her differently and returned their focus to my presentation.

I've had ADD adults report that they recognize that they interrupt other people. Therefore, they've learned to shut-up. Because ideas or topics are constantly bombarding their thoughts, they do not follow a conversation as closely as it appears. In other words, they are not able to understand an entire conversation. They may appear to understand because they are sitting quietly. The reason they are sitting quietly is because they don't know what to say. They are just disguising their confusion and trying to act polite.

Difficulty dealing with paperwork

This may include personal papers as well as work situations. At home, they may have difficulties and forget to record checks they have written. The non-ADD spouse may complain of this trait often.

In a work situation, paperwork may be very frustrating to them because it requires concentration and sitting for long periods of time. Most people with ADD are good at working with their hands, but not sitting and dealing with paperwork. Consequently, many people with ADD gravitate toward occupations in which paperwork is reduced to a minimum. Many ADD people enjoy the outdoors or the freedom of movement provided by some occupations. Obviously, there are exceptions to the rule. There are some ADD people who work in professions that require very little physical activity. What you must remember is that their mind may be extremely active when they are working. Therefore, they are not being as inactive as it may appear.

Disorganized lifestyle

Many people with ADD are often late for appointments or they are a stickler for being on time to the point of being there extremely early. They may recognize that they are often late, so they get there early, sometimes several hours early. In working situations, they may be unprepared and wait until the last minute to complete a task.

Takes on too many projects

Many people with ADD have a variety of interests. Unfortunately, they may get started on one and never complete it because, all of a sudden, they've become interested in another task. This is very similar to how they were as youngsters. They never played with one toy for any length of time. They hardly completed tasks. This trait carries over into adulthood and may cause some difficulties in their job, depending on what their occupation entails.

Many ADD adults are extremely intelligent, but they may not achieve as much as their peers. This is usually related to their inability to concentrate, follow through on tasks, low frustration tolerance, and disorganization. Again, they may be more intelligent than their peers, but the traits and symptoms of ADD keep them from achieving as much as they could. They also may have to work more hours than others to do the same amount of work. They may appear to be workaholics or conscientious, but in reality they can't do things as quickly as others.

Low stress tolerance

Most people with ADD have very strong emotions. This applies to all emotions: anger, depression, happiness, sex. Whatever the average person feels, the ADD person feels stronger. Therefore, when the ADD adult is faced with a stressful situation, they may not be able to cope as easily as others. Consequently, they may become discouraged more quickly than others. Another way of saying this is that they overreact to stress.

Is seen as untrustworthy

Many ADD adults have a poor memory, and they are impulsive. Therefore, they make promises they don't keep. They either impulsively decide to do something else, or they totally forget. This obviously irritates other people and makes others draw conclusions as to why this person did this. One of the common conclusions that a spouse draws is that they are uncaring and inconsiderate. To summarize, the ADD person can't be relied upon to carry through on what they promise. The traits of ADD are responsible for them being irresponsible.

However, there are times that they say they will do something and purposely don't do it. We may never know <u>exactly</u> what they were thinking, but sometimes they misinterpret the discussion. They may not understand that they made a <u>solid</u> commitment. To them, it was an <u>optional</u> commitment. To get them to keep a commitment, you may have to emphasize the importance and remind them often in order to get them to follow through.

Letter

Dear Mr. Hunsucker,

You asked readers to write to you of their experiences growing up with undiagnosed ADD. I feel as though my life was put on "pause" 26 years ago when I was 15, and only began again 2 years ago at age 39, when I began to take medication for what was diagnosed as a severe, chronic anxiety disorder. In between, I dropped out of high school (although I had an I.Q. score of 130), turned to alcohol, married and divorced twice, took Valium for 6 years, was diagnosed with depression, as having a prolapsed mitral valve, and became an agoraphobic for 5 years.

All that time, I knew there was something physically wrong with me, no matter how my family, friends, and doctors tried to convince me that my problems were "in my head." I couldn't learn the way other people did. I was always "in a fog." My husband used to say I had permanent "jet lag." If someone spoke to me, it was as though they were speaking another language.

Yes, I could hear the words, but by the time I put the words together in my mind to form a thought, the person speaking was so far ahead of me that I was lost. I gave up listening and became frustrated and angry. This didn't happen just occasionally; I lived this 24 hours a day for 26 years. By the time I was 34, I was convinced that I either didn't have much longer to live, or at the very least, I was going to be insane for the rest of my life.

For people who think that this disorder only affects a person academically, you don't know how wrong you are. It affects every aspect of your life, every hour, every day, until you are treated with medication. When my teenager started to exhibit symptoms, I immediately took him to my doctor, who put him on medication that very day. I wasn't going to let my son suffer one minute longer than he had to. I'm so sorry that I didn't recognize that he had the disorder 4 years earlier, but at that time, I was still suffering from it myself. I apologize frequently to him for the couple of years he lost, but I thank God it was only a few years and not a lifetime, as it was with me.

The best way to describe my life, and my son's life, after diagnosis and treatment is NORMAL, wonderfully, normally, NORMAL. I'd like to tell every person who has ever been diagnosed as suffering from "anxiety" or "nerves," please suspect attention deficit disorder before you allow yourself to be put on tranquilizers. Just because you're an adult, doesn't mean you can't be ADD.

Sherri

Author's Response

Please note the things that she pointed out:

- Dropped out of high school
- Was misdiagnosed as having several different "psychological" problems
- High intelligence
- Her son inherited it and was diagnosed
- Abused alcohol
- Trouble maintaining relationships

She notes that when others spoke to her, it took her awhile to figure out a response.

This is an important point. Many people misinterpret an ADD person's response to questions or conversations. She, like others with ADD, have confused thinking. This makes it hard for them to follow a conversation. They often interrupt others. They recognize that if they don't say what is on their mind right then, they will forget. Obviously, others misinterpret this as being rude.

Some ADD people "mask" this unclear thinking by doing exactly the opposite. They say nothing, but they don't comprehend or understand the topic of conversation. Again, others often misinterpret their lack of response. They may be seen as not caring about what is being discussed, or they may be seen as "good listeners." Both of these conclusions are incorrect. The true reason is that they have trouble following the conversation.

ADD children often ask off-the-wall questions in the classroom. They may ask a question that the teacher answered 5 minutes earlier. This embarrasses them, especially when their peers laugh or make comments. From incidents such as this, they may learn to "keep their mouth shut," even if they don't understand what the teacher said or what directions were given. As adults, they may continue using this method of coping.

CHAPTER 7

FAMILY RELATIONSHIPS

At this point, I would like to say that my purpose in writing books on ADD is to convince people to get treated with medication. Each section of this book may have negative aspects to it. These are mentioned for positive reasons. If you, the reader, understand what untreated ADD causes in a person's life, you may be motivated to suggest treatment for those with ADD.

This section of my book may motivate someone to seek treatment more so than any other section. Most people do things for their family before they do anything for themselves, especially when it comes to treating ADD. Hopefully, I can show the ADD adult that their untreated ADD is negatively affecting the most important people in their life. Therefore, treatment may help their family as well as themselves.

Every person who lives under the same roof with the untreated ADD adult is affected by the symptoms of ADD, especially children.

Many ADD adults are moody, impulsive, forgetful and unpredictable. In essence, these are the traits of a "dysfunctional" parent. Without going into detail, it's obvious that a child who must deal with this kind of adult is going to be negatively affected. As a matter of fact, the ADD adult's behavior may be described as emotionally abusive.

The ADD adult is a nice person when they are not "over-stimulated" or placed in a stressful situation. Unfortunately, children will always put parents in stressful situations. For the ADD adult, they may not respond as the "average" parent would respond. They usually over-react.

In extreme cases, ADD adults may become physically abusive because of their temper outbursts.

The parent who doesn't have ADD may become the peace maker and intervene when the ADD adult "blows up". Arguments between the spouses usually erupt over disciplinary methods. More often than not, the ADD spouse is wrong and the non-ADD spouse is right, in their parenting opinions. Obviously, this is not true all of the time but, because of their over-reaction to events, ADD adults often choose the wrong response.

The non-ADD spouse may end up seeking therapy (usually the wife) because of the stress involved in living with the ADD spouse. Most ADD adults are intelligent and manipulative. Therefore, they may be able to convince the non-ADD spouse that they are the ones with the problem.

If the ADD adult has a child with ADD, this complicates the picture. The ADD adult could be harmful to this child, especially emotionally. On the other hand, there are some cases in which the adult may be of help because they are able to identify with the struggles the child is experiencing. How the ADD adult responds is dependent upon their personality and their particular "type" of ADD.

The more volatile ADD parent is impatient and may become extremely hostile with the ADD child. The ADD child may also have a bad temper and respond with anger and hostility. Since the adult is larger, they usually win the confrontation by the use of force.

I won't go into detail as to what can happen when two ADD people confront each other. However, use your imagination and visualize two people who are stubborn, with a short and bad temper, who are impulsive, and are prone to act out their behavior. This combination spells trouble, especially when the ADD child is a teenager.

On the other extreme, is the ADD parent who doesn't follow up close enough on their child. This ADD adult may be so disorganized and forgetful that they can't keep up with the everyday stresses of being a parent. They may not be as attentive to the emotional well being of their child as other parents. This is not because they don't want to, it's just that they don't pick up the "cues" and subtle messages the child gives. ADD people are often slow in putting information together and finding solutions to problems. They don't pick up on these messages.

Again, if this parent has an ADD child, the impact on the child will be negative. ADD children need more structure, more follow up and more attention paid to their emotional well being than the non-ADD child. Therefore, having a parent who is unable to do this will be detrimental to the child.

LIVING WITH AN ADD SPOUSE

Living with an ADD spouse is difficult. They usually have traits that go from one extreme to the other. What good traits they have, are probably great. The problem is with their bad traits, because these also fall at the extreme. In other words, whatever negative traits they have, they are probably very bad.

To give some examples: people with ADD have strong emotions. When they get angry, they may become violent. When they are in a loving mood, they can be the most charming and romantic person alive. This usually confuses the non-ADD spouse.

This usually causes the non-ADD spouse to weigh the pros and cons of getting a divorce. The positive traits are so positive that they know they would never find another person like this. However, the negative traits are so bad that they know that they can't live like this forever.

The negative traits, such as anger, may occur very seldom. Therefore, the decision to get a divorce may be delayed and postponed for a number of years. The non-ADD spouse knows that if they could get rid of these negative traits, their spouse would be the most wonderful person in the world. This is often true. The problem is, nothing has been successful in stopping these negative traits because no one knows they have ADD.

When an ADD spouse is properly treated, the marital relationship often improves.

Not every ADD spouse has a bad temper, but these are the ones that usually have the hardest time maintaining a marriage.

"Lesser" problems of an ADD spouse involves their disorganized approach to life and irresponsible habits. This puts pressure on a marriage because the other spouse often mis-interprets the actions of the ADD spouse. Inconsiderate or uncaring are the most common mis-interpretations.

The problems in ADD marriages are often more extreme than those of the non-ADD couple. Most couples have arguments over money or being inconsiderate. However, the ADD couple may have more problems in these areas than most people.

The non-ADD spouse may become extremely frustrated because when they complain, they are told that this is just "normal". Again, others don't understand the degree to which this person is referring. It's true that these events occur in all marriages, but not to the same degree.

Those with ADD often have trouble maintaining marriages. Their impulsiveness, lack of responsible behavior and bad tempers are the major traits that cause the problems. (Drug and alcohol abuse and other addictive behaviors are common to those with ADD. Therefore, these may be the identified problem, but ADD is the un-identified cause).

It's unfortunate that ADD adults don't receive treatment because they often have abilities that others don't. Unfortunately, they are unable to capitalize on them. If you have an ADD spouse, I strongly suggest they get treatment.

Some spouses may not want the ADD spouse to receive treatment. The reason for this is sometimes selfish. Many people with ADD are somewhat naive and easily manipulated. If they are properly treated, the other spouse may view the changes as negative. In other words, the ADD spouse no longer has an overly emotional response to arguments or events and is able to "think things through". This may lead them to making different decisions or confronting their spouse. In other words, the other spouse loses their ability to control the ADD spouse.

Divorce and Child Custody

Because the Divorce rate of those with ADD is higher than the average, this section is essential. I've been to court for several child custody cases involving ADD.

Here is a quick list of the most common situations I've encountered:

Child has ADD and is on medication
↓
Mother has custody of the child
↓
Father has ADD but, doesn't know it, accept it, or believe it. Therefore he is untreated
↓
Father doesn't like his child taking medication
↓
His son does well when he visits with him on weekends or in the summer. Therefore, the father blames his son's problems (academic or behavioral) on his ex-wife and her poor parenting skills
↓

The Father's attorney has a good case because society <u>always</u> blames the parent for a child's problems
↓
Therefore, they file for custody
↓
The Mother is at a disadvantage because her ADD child has both behavioral and academic problems (due to ADD)
↓
The lack of knowledge about ADD among professionals means the mother and her attorney can't find an "expert" who can clearly explain ADD and it's affect on the child and parent.
↓
The opposing attorney can find numerous professionals who will blame the mother's parenting skills simply because professionals can't find any other explanation for the child's problems. They don't understand ADD.
↓
The father wins custody
↓
He refuses to give his son medication
↓
The child performs well for 2 or 3 months
↓
The child then starts having the <u>same</u> problems he had when he was with his mother
↓
The <u>untreated</u> ADD Father, who has a bad temper, becomes harsh and tries to correct his son's problems by being very strict
↓
The child continues to have problems and may start rebelling against the father
↓
The father continues to push him, or seeks counseling
↓
The professional to whom they go, doesn't understand ADD and how it affects the child
↓
Therefore, the professional assumes ADD has nothing to do with the problem so he starts <u>counseling</u> as the treatment
↓

The child may now want to live with his mother again
because of the stress he's encountering
↓

The Mother may know what the problem is but has no
control over getting her child treated with medication
↓

The Father, in essence, is re-learning what the mother
already knows
↓

Unfortunately, this "on the job training", is causing the child
to suffer
↓

By the time the child is a teenager, his ADD may never be
suspected as the reason for his problems
↓

Other relatives may try to "rescue" the child by allowing
him to live with them
↓

They assume that both the parents are the reason for the
child's problems
↓

The child again may do well for a short period of time
↓

At some point he starts having problems, but because of his
age, the problems are different from those encountered at an
early age.
↓

At this point, another relative may try to rescue the child
↓

They assume the same thing everyone else assumed: "It's the
fault of the adults with whom they live"
↓

This pattern of switching from relative to relative may be
repeated over and over but the child never receives help for
his ADD
↓

The End (of this explanation, not this child's problems)

The person who suffers from this, is the child. The
father filed for custody, thinking he was doing what was

best for his child. His intentions were honorable. I have no doubt of this.

Unfortunately, he hurt his child more than he will ever know. The Father's ADD also plays an important role in this process.

They are often stubborn and hold <u>strong grudges</u> against their ex-spouse. I underlined <u>strong</u>, to emphasize the <u>degree</u> of emotion that the ADD person often feels. They may feel so much resentment toward their ex, that they will go to the "ends of the earth" to discredit them.

Again, this person's ADD (the chemical imbalance) is the primary reason for their strong emotions.

By writing this section, I hope to show those who have custody battles over an ADD child, how much harm can be done to the child.

Parents, before discounting ADD as being part of the problem, I suggest you read some of my other books. You need to understand how serious it is.

Unfortunately, most people want to prove that their opinion of their ex-spouse is correct. Therefore, they often have "tunnel vision" and concentrate on their own emotions and not the childs. They want to "get back at", their ex.

[COMMENT]

Attorneys and judges have damaged thousands of children (who grew up to be adults) because of their lack of knowledge about ADD. They made decisions based on incomplete information.

To all of the attorneys who deal with child custody cases, I offer you a suggestion:

Always . . . . yes, Always, consider the possibility of ADD playing a part in your case. Not just within the child, but within the siblings or parents.

Why do I say this? Because you are dealing with a special population of people (those divorcing, or who have a child who is having academic or behavioral problems). There are more ADD people in this special population than in other populations. Therefore, it should be the first thing investigated.

WOMEN WHO HAVE AN ADD BROTHER
How This Affects Their Views Of Men

Before we start talking specifically about how living with an ADD sibling affects a person, we need to understand some general information about how all of us develop our attitudes and values.

We know that the people you are around affect and mold your view of the world. The views and attitudes of family members affect how you see yourself and others. How we are treated as we grow up affects how we treat others and how we feel we should be treated. My basic point in this section is; the female who is reared with an ADD brother, will view people differently than the female who was reared with a non-ADD brother.

When I say she will view people differently than

others, I am specifically talking about her view of men. This is extremely important, because the men she will choose will be determined by what she accepts as "normal" male behavior. If she was reared with an ADD brother, she may accept behavior in men that other females would not accept.

A sibling with ADD thinks and acts differently than the average sibling. Perhaps a more correct way of phrasing this is, their reactions to situations are more extreme than most. When they get angry, they may get extremely angry. When they get their feelings hurt, they may feel <u>destroyed</u>. If they want attention, they may want an excessive amount of attention. In other words, they do exactly the same thing that every other sibling does, but they are prone to do it to the extreme.

Let us consider the situation in which the ADD brother gets into an argument with his younger sister. We can use any age group.

Because the ADD brother is impulsive, gets extremely mad and can't express himself well, he may respond with physical aggression. People with ADD often have a high tolerance for pain, and have trouble recognizing that others don't. Therefore, when he responds physically, he may be extremely rough on his sister and not realize how badly he is hurting her. His treatment of her, if committed by a parent, might be considered physical or emotional abuse.

As you can imagine, if this kind of treatment occurs over a number of years, this girl will have experienced a great deal of emotional and physical trauma. It will also affect her self-esteem. She may develop such resentment toward her brother that it may never be healed. She may treasure the moment that he leaves the home. In fact, she may leave at an early age just to get away from him.

Because she is weaker and has little control over how he treats her, she may look for outside help. This means that she looks to the parents for relief. Unfortunately, what she doesn't understand is that her brother has ADD and his behavior is not within the control of the parents. They may try to control him but they will have very little success.

Another thing that she may not understand is that her brother gets into more trouble than the average child. Because of this, the parents may have to overlook some of his mis-behaviors because they get tired of trying to punish him for every infraction. Witnessing the leniency of the parents toward her brother, she may draw her own conclusion as to why this is occurring.

One conclusion she is likely to make is that they favor him, otherwise they wouldn't allow him to act this way. This may cause resentment toward the parents. She may feel that they could make him behave if they would.

Resentment may also build when they punish her for being 5 minutes late, while her brother receives less punishment for staying out 2 or 3 hours late. She sees this as unfair, and it is. But again, the parents have discovered that they have very little control over him and confronting him may cause a bigger fight than just letting it go.

Needless to say, by the time she is an adult, she may resent both the parents and the ADD sibling.

Subconsciously, it may affect her choice of men. She may marry a man similar to her brother. If he was somewhat abusive, this means that she may tolerate a man who is more aggressive than the average person.

I'm not saying that every female who is reared with an ADD sibling will have a distorted view of men. Some will not. It may actually help some women know what kind of man to avoid.

You must remember that the people with whom I've dealt are in a special population. Therefore, the people who come to visit me, were not coming to tell me how great their lives were. They were having problems.

I have come in contact with women who married an ADD man but also had an ADD brother. This amazed me. I've also seen women who married an ADD man, got divorced, and re-married another ADD man.

This is not as unusual as it may seem because most people gravitate toward certain personality types. Even when you think a person is much different from the last one you married or dated, they are probably more similar than you realize.

People with ADD gravitate toward others who have ADD. This is why many ADD women marry ADD men. There are ten times as many men with ADD as women, so there is a large number of non-ADD women married to ADD men.

ADD is hereditary. When two people have a child, that child now carries the ADD gene. Even if one of the parents has ADD (a child can have ADD even if a parent doesn't), not every child will have ADD. ADD may not show up again until this parent has a grandchild.

In other words, a non-ADD person's "blood line" has basically stopped when they marry a person whose blood line contains ADD. This means that any off-spring could be born with ADD. To say it another way: the number of "blood lines" with ADD are increasing, and the number of "blood lines" without ADD are decreasing.

The number of people with ADD is increasing every year. Think about this.

SIBLING RIVALRY

This section is devoted to relationships between the ADD sibling and non-ADD sibling. The relationship between these two individuals is often much more intense and difficult than that of the average sibling relationship.

I hope this section increases the understanding between those who have had such a relationship, especially if the ADD sibling was not known to have had ADD.

Many of these siblings grow up hating or resenting each other without understanding that ADD was the major cause of their inability to be friends.

The volatile relationship between these siblings is the extreme example of sibling rivalry. Books written on sibling rivalry often use extreme examples to demonstrate their point. By giving these extreme examples, they feel that they are proving their point or theory. In a sense, they are, but what they don't seem to understand is that one of the siblings is in a "special population". In other words, one sibling has ADD and the other doesn't. This means that the ADD sibling is going to be much different than the non-ADD sibling. This also means that they will be treated differently by the parents.

Again, what I'm pointing out is how professionals mis-interpret behaviors because they don't understand ADD.

A common explanation of sibling rivalry is that the parents show favoritism to one child because they make better grades or have better behavior. This "explanation" suggests that it is "the parents" fault for showing this favoritism. It implies that the sibling rivalry arose because one child observed this favoritism and therefore became jealous. To vent their feelings of rejection and jealousy, they became behavior problems or did poorly in school.

I find this explanation superficial.

I have worked with hundreds of families and I see ADD and non-ADD sibling rivalry often. Therefore, I feel that the classic cases of sibling rivalry that professionals write about, are examples of an ADD and non-ADD sibling. This rivalry should not be interpreted as typical. Unfortunately, it appears that the field of psychology has unwittingly accepted this A-typical sibling rivalry as the model for the typical behavior between siblings. Once again, I feel that this is a mis-interpretation of the research data.

I would now like to give my explanation as to "why" the parents seem to show favoritism toward one child.

It's actually very simple: one has ADD and the other doesn't. It's almost impossible to treat them the same because the ADD child doesn't respond or act the same as other children. Therefore, they <u>have</u> to be treated differently. The <u>reason</u> for this different treatment is interpreted differently by the siblings.

The ADD child may feel that the parents' discipline him more than his sibling, for no good reason. He is unable to see how his behavior leads to his frequent punishment. He only sees that he gets punished more often than his sibling.

On the other hand, the non-ADD sibling may harbor resentment toward the parents because he feels they don't punish the ADD sibling enough. He observes the parents ignoring negative behaviors of his sibling that they do not ignore in him. For example: The ADD sibling may not be punished for making C's or D's on his report card while the non-ADD sibling gets punished for these grades. This is seen as unfair by the non-ADD child.

Oddly enough, both siblings are <u>correct</u> in their observation that the parents are inconsistent. However, both are <u>incorrect</u> in their interpretation of <u>why</u> the parents are inconsistent. (Professionals who complain of this inconsistency apparently don't know that one child has ADD and the other doesn't. If he did, he would understand why the parents are inconsistent).

As stated earlier, it's impossible to treat the ADD child exactly like the non-ADD child. Even if you do treat them the same (ie: punish them for the same things), the ADD child will probably not see it that way. They interpret their environment differently than others.

When this ADD child reaches adulthood, they have a view of their up-bringing that is not totally accurate. Therefore, when they tell others about their "difficult" childhood, they are reporting their "distorted" view. They don't necessarily do this to intentionally criticize their parents or other family members. They merely report their interpretation of why they were treated as they were.

On the other hand, some ADD adults blame their childhood treatment for their current problems. They may be searching for an explanation as to why they are having problems maintaining a job or relationship. They may also be looking for an explanation as to why they are depressed, have a bad temper, or do things impulsively. Since they have no idea that they have ADD, this is not even considered as a possible explanation. Instead, they usually turn to what most of us turn to; our past. Since our past basically entails our childhood, we focus on those who had the biggest influence on us at that time. This means we focus upon the parents and how they treated us. This is why parents are often blamed, unfairly.

IT'S NOT THE PARENTS' FAULT

ADD is <u>more common</u> than bad parents.

I also say that ADD is more common as an explanation for criminal behavior and alcohol/drug abuse than is bad parenting.

I've always found it curious that parents are often blamed for their child's problems but, not their

<u>successes</u>.

I've also found it curious that parents who are criticized as being bad parents, often have other children who have no behavior or emotional problems. This is an extremely important point and I want to dwell upon it for a few moments.

Professionals have never been able to give a <u>satisfactory</u> answer as to why this occurs. They often give the usual psychological mumbo-jumbo explanation that sounds good, but on closer analysis, proves to be weak.

For example: The most common explanation given for the big difference between siblings, is that all people are different.

I agree with this. However, this statement does not address the <u>real</u> question. The question is, why is there such a <u>big</u> difference between one sibling and the other.

If professionals still insist that this dramatic difference is due to individual differences, I will agree once again. But, they still have not answered the main question: what <u>is</u> this individual difference?

I not only agree that this big difference is due to individual differences, but I'm willing to be <u>specific</u> and state what this individual difference is.

The individual difference is <u>ADD</u>. One has ADD and the other doesn't. It's that simple. I've seen this hundreds of times. Once the ADD sibling was treated with medication, the <u>big</u> difference was reduced.

Most professionals are such poor thinkers that they don't see the contradiction in the psychological principles and theories that they've been taught.

Professionals who directly or indirectly blame the parents for a child's problems don't understand how illogical their arguments are. For example; when they mention <u>individual differences</u> as an explanation for the other children having no problems, they have <u>contradicted</u> themselves. They have <u>changed</u> the topic.

The topic started out as focusing upon the <u>parenting skills</u> of the parents. When they start mentioning the <u>individual differences</u> of the children, they are merely confirming my point. They are saying that there is "something" <u>different</u> about the child who has academic, behavior, or emotional problems. Once again, I agree. I say that this "something" is often ADD. As you can see, the discussion of the parents is no longer relevant.

Another popular explanation for one child having problems while the others have none, is that he is "acting out the dysfunction of the family". In other words, the professional suggests that the family is really "messed up" but they don't know it. This is another example of professionals "over psychologizing". They are looking for an explanation as to why there is such a dramatic difference between the children and blaming the parents, or the entire family, is all they can come up with. (If they understood ADD, they would understand that there is another explanation that is more reasonable). Even when a professional concludes that this child is <u>"acting out the dysfunction of the family"</u>, they still haven't answered the primary question:

Why is this <u>particular child</u> acting out the family

dysfunction and not the others? Once again, the answer reverts back to the discussion of <u>individual</u> differences. This is a circular argument. The professionals never give you a logical answer. They merely take your <u>question</u>, re-arrange the words, and make a <u>statement</u> out of your question. Most people don't catch this trick. As a matter of fact, the professionals who do this don't do it intentionally. They have always done it and no one has ever confronted them or challenged the logic behind their reasoning. Therefore, they've never had to analyze their statements.

As I've said many times before, the majority of people in the mental health profession are "feelers" and not "thinkers". When they do "think", they are usually thinking of emotions (often their own).

Most people do not have a great deal of experience with arguing against professionals. Therefore, very few people are able to think <u>fast</u> enough to see these contradictions. These type of discussions are often in situations where the professional has total control of the environment.

The non-professional is either in an unfamiliar environment and doesn't feel comfortable enough to think fast, or they are not allotted enough time to give their views. Also, the professional often gets the last word by drawing the discussion to an end.

This is why professionals never have to confront or answer questions that challenge their thinking.

SEXUAL ACTIVITY AND ADD

People with ADD often have an unusual sex drive. They have an extremely <u>strong</u> sex drive or an extremely <u>weak</u> sex drive. Both extremes can cause problems.

Sex is a strong motivator for many people. Therefore, the ADD spouse who has a strong sex drive may be very satisfying to the other spouse even if they are hard to tolerate outside of the bedroom. This sexual satisfaction can often cause a spouse to delay their decision to get a divorce, regardless of how bad the relationship is in other areas. Needless to say, the person with ADD is often more liberal and willing to experiment. This also makes them more appealing to the other spouse. It's quite possible that the person with ADD has also learned that sex can be used to control and prolong a relationship that is failing in other areas. This may work for a period of time, but the negative aspects of the relationship will eventually outweigh the positives of sex.

Because ADD people have few areas in which they have been successful, sex often plays a much bigger role in their life than it should. This is one area in which they can feel successful and also reduce their constant state of tension. This is why young ADD teenagers are prone to become parents and give up the child for adoption. (Remember, 4 times as many adopted children have ADD as non-adopted).

Understanding the reason for the extreme differences in sex drives between ADD people merely requires an understanding of ADD (a chemical imbalance).

Most people with ADD experience extremes in emotions, pain, sugar intake, or amount of time to make decisions.

To understand this is rather <u>simple</u>. The chemical in the brain that relays the "message" about one of these areas, relays the "wrong message".

For example, let us discuss <u>pain</u>. One ADD person may have a very high tolerance while another has a very low tolerance. The chemical merely relays a different message for each of these people. Why? I don't know. However, the medication works for both people in the same way. It relays the correct message.

Now, back to the difference in sex drive. I used pain tolerance as an example because oddly enough, it plays a role in the discussion of sex.

Pain tolerance actually translates to <u>"tactual sensitivity"</u>. In other words, <u>feeling what you touch</u> or <u>what touches you</u>. One person can feel a very light touch (very sensitive), while another person can't feel a touch unless a great deal of pressure is exerted. (This may actually vary from day to day. It may even vary from one body part to another.)

To get to the point about sex, one ADD person may have an above average sex drive while another ADD person may be below average.

One ADD person may require a great deal of stimulation to reach orgasm while another may require very little.

Please note: Having a weak or strong sex drive is not related to how sensitive to stimulation a person may be. They can have a very weak <u>sex drive</u> but be very sensitive to stimulation. They may have an orgasm easily, but getting them to <u>have sex</u> becomes the problem. They just don't show a lot of interest until they are actually in the act.

Again, medication helps the people with either extreme. It allows a person to feel their sex drive within the "average range", and allows them to become more or less sensitive to stimulation (depending on which extreme they experience).

In summary, the sex drive and amount of stimulation needed to reach an orgasm, is dependent upon the type of <u>"chemical message"</u> the ADD person receives.

I've talked with many ADD male adults, who have reported similar sexual experiences. Many of them can now look back and see that they were <u>"over sexed"</u>. Several reported that they were afraid that they might become a rapist. They thought about sex constantly, or engaged in it (alone or with someone) as often as possible.

[This raises some interesting questions regarding the traditional theory of rape being an act of violence and not sex, at least in some instances.]

After medication, many of these individuals no longer had a strong sex drive. It became more "normal" and healthy. Those who had a low sex drive initially, experienced an increase.

Homosexuality and ADD

I may have more to say on this topic in later books, but I would at least like to make you curious by noting an interesting study.

A study was done on male homosexual prostitutes in New York City. The findings were incredible. 80% were found to be hyperactive (ADD). These symptoms had been present since childhood. 68% had been involved in alcohol or drug abuse at some point.

These numbers are extremely high when compared to the average population. I'll not draw any final conclusions based on this one study but I believe this area needs to be studied in depth.

However, based on what you have read in this book, you can see how several symptoms of ADD could combine in such a way that may result in a person adopting this life-style.

Again, I'll not go into detail at this point because there are a lot of other factors that must be discussed before conclusions are drawn. Therefore, I'll stop my discussion at this point.

Letter

Dear Mr. Hunsucker:

I have recently purchased and read your book "ADD - Attention Deficit Disorder". I found it to be extremely enlightening and helpful. It was stated in the book that you would be writing on the subject of ADD and the adult. This is where my interest is at this time.

I have a 26 year old son who was placed on medication at the age of 6 for learning difficulties in the first grade. He was on it for about a year and improved not only at school but at home. At that time, 20 years ago, little was known, or seemed to be known about this disorder. A "learning disability" seemed to be the diagnosis and I was led to believe that it would disappear by adolescence. He managed to go to college and now holds down a very good job, although his impulsive nature causes him some problems at times.

I did not know when this son was six years of age that this disorder was inherited nor that it was a chemical imbalance. My question of concern now that I am learning much more about the disorder, involves my husband (57 years of age). I feel quite sure that he has had ADD from childhood. From what I have gleaned about his childhood, and adolescence and into his twenties, all of the signs were there, but of course no diagnosis or even questions that his problems might have been physiological were made. The symptoms in adolescence led to alcohol abuse into his adult life. He has solved the alcohol problems to the extent that he knows that he cannot drink and that it only created more problems for him. While he has done very well in his career, his social and family responsibilities cause him even more problems. Talking therapy has helped to bolster his confidence in himself, but as far as treating the condition on a long term basis it did not help at all. He has never been on any kind of medication.

I feel that he could find his life so much easier and certainly have a happier outlook on so many things if he could be tested and diagnosed, if this is the problem. From all that I have read, he appears to fit all of the signs of an ADD adult (and past child). If not for our older son having been diagnosed, it would have never entered my mind, until now, that I find that this is a hereditary thing. (We have two other children, neither of whom have ever shown any signs of ADD.)

I am very interested in your book on ADD in adults. Has it been published?

Thank you,

Betty

Author's Response

This is an example of how different ADD adults can be. Her husband has been successful in his career, but his social and family life has not been successful. Some ADD adults have the opposite experience. Their social and family life may be good but they cannot achieve in their occupation.

He went to "talk" therapy for his problem and had no success. This is a complaint I have against my profession. Professionals are so ignorant of this disorder that it never crosses their minds that ADD could be the problem. Most professionals don't know that ADD occurs in adults and that ADD is one of the biggest causes of people seeking counseling. It seems that they only see the immediate problem and don't suspect that an underlying problem like ADD led to their current situation. They also don't investigate the person's childhood to see if there were symptoms evident at that time.

They also didn't consider hereditary factors. His son was diagnosed at age 6. This should have made the therapist suspicious and ask questions about the adult's background.

His wife mentioned an important point in her last sentence. She pointed out that they have two other children who have absolutely no signs of ADD. In other words, there is a definite difference between an ADD child and the average child, even when they live in the same environment, with the same parents.

The reason I mention this is to show how wrong many professionals are when they blame the parents or environment for a child's problem. Why is it that the two other children didn't have academic or behavior problems? The answer is, individual differences! The specific individual difference is ADD; one had it and the other two did not.

CHAPTER 8

WORK

<u>Research</u> indicates the following about ADD adults:

- **They changed jobs more often than most people.**
- **They had more part time jobs than others.**
- **They do not complete their tasks as well as others.**
- **They have trouble working independently.**
- **They don't get along well with supervisors.**
- **They don't perform their jobs as well as others.**

I'm now going to combine these traits in a practical manner. In other words, I'm going to explain how they interrelate and apply to real life.

ADD adults change jobs more often than others for a variety of reasons. ADD adults get "bored" with doing one job for a period of time. This boredom is due to their need to constantly be doing or learning something.

Once they learn a job, they may not stick with it long enough to become successful. Once they learn the basics, and there is no longer variety in the job, they are ready to move to another job where they have to re-learn the specifics of the job. This may be mis-interpreted as a desire to learn when it really represents their inability to have patience and stick with one job, even if it does get boring or routine.

Another reason they change jobs often is due to their inability to get along with their employers.

Oddly enough, many people with ADD are charming and very good at giving a good first impression. Therefore, they are able to get hired more easily than others. After employers find out what they are like, they are no longer charming. In other words, they are more "talk than action". When it's time to produce, they don't live up to expectations. This is similar to what parents observe in ADD children. They are good at making friends, but they aren't good at keeping them.

Some ADD adults work long hours and seem to be workaholics. This is often due to their inability to do the same work others do in the allotted time. They may work after hours when there are fewer distractions in order to complete tasks. Although it may appear that they are conscientious, it may be that they are unable to do things as quickly as others. Because they are disorganized, more time is required to get their work area organized or to get themselves into the "mood."

The ADD person who works long hours, may feel that they are more loyal or more valuable than others. If they do not receive a promotion, they may feel slighted and quit their jobs. Of course when they tell their friends or relatives why they left, they will point out the long hours they put in for this company. What they don't report is what I mentioned earlier. The extra time they put in was due to their inability to be productive in the allotted time.

You can see, that if this person is paid by the hour, they will cost the company more than the other workers.

Some ADD people work hard but accomplish little. It not only takes them more time to do their job, they also require more detailed explanations from the employer. They may have others help them, just to keep up.

What usually happens after a few months, is that they start looking for explanations as to why they have to work so hard. The most common reason they come up with is that their employer is "expecting" too much from them.

(This is very similar to what ADD children do when they have trouble completing tasks. They start blaming others for their inability to perform. This is a defense mechanism that allows them to protect their self-image. If they blame themselves, they may become depressed and lose their self worth.)

Many ADD adults don't recognize how their inability to concentrate and pay attention causes work problems.

I know of an ADD adult who was fired because he copied the wrong numbers on forms. (This is a problem ADD children sometimes have. It appears to be "dyslexia" but it isn't.) He had to transfer 6 digits from a box to an order form. Because of his ADD, he re-arranged the order of the digits. This caused a discrepancy which cost the company a lot of money. Needless to say, a person who makes a large number of mistakes will eventually lose their job.

Many people with ADD also have problems distinguishing between the trivial aspects of their job and the most important. (Again, this is directly related to ADD children and their comprehension problems. They often have trouble distinguishing between what's important information and what's not. Consequently, they do poorly on tests because they study the wrong information.) The adult may spend a great deal of time on unimportant projects while those with a higher priority are delayed. An employer will not tolerate this for a long period of time.

Because ADD adults have a low tolerance for frustration, they may not be able to handle the same amount of stress as others. In other words, they may require more time to "cool off", or "settle down" after a stressful event. This will cost the employer because time is wasted while they are "cooling off". If a stressful event occurs at home or work 2 or 3 times a week, you can see how this will negatively impact the company's performance or productivity.

OTHER JOB RELATED PROBLEMS OF ADD ADULTS

- **Their views on certain matters seem to change from day to day.**

This is usually due to the fact that their first decision was not well thought out or was somewhat "impulsive". In this case, impulsive is not meant in the traditional sense. ADD adults, because they have trouble incorporating all the needed information quickly, may make decisions before considering other pertinent information. They may know about this pertinent information but not "remember" it when it is time to make a decision. Therefore, it may appear that they made an "impulsive" decision.

They may "remember' this information a day later and because of this "new" information, their decision on the matter may change dramatically. Others may interpret this change of view as bizarre. The ADD adult may have been extremely excited about something one day, but after having time to think about it in "depth", they are no longer excited.

Most ADD adults are extremely intelligent. Consequently, they can come up with innovative ideas. Although this is admirable, they often overlook the more practical or subtle realities of a job or task. They are "dreamers" and not "doers".

- **They have a variety of creative and innovative ideas but never follow through to make them happen.**

Most Add people are extremely intelligent and creative. Consequently, they can come up with great ideas, but cannot "stick with" something long enough to see it completed. Ironically, this creativity and almost endless number of ideas is one of the reasons they can't "stick with" one task.

ADD people are constantly active, but not in the physical sense. Ideas and thoughts come to them almost constantly. This makes it hard for them to concentrate on anything for a long period of time. They have to put forth an excessive amount of effort to "fight off" the constant bombardment of ideas, auditory distractions, and visual distractions.

This is why they have trouble sticking with an endeavor over a long period of time. They forget, or lose sight of their long term goal. As a matter of fact, they usually think of short term gain and not long term. They may have the best of intentions when they start a long term project but the symptoms of ADD keep them from completing it. Therefore, they never follow through.

- **They have trouble organizing their time and consequently are often late for appointments.**

Because of their disorganization, someone may have to organize their time for them. They may recognize that they are disorganized and try to compensate for it by having lists or a brief case organizer. Unfortunately, they often lose the list or briefcase.

I've known adults who bought expensive organizers but never got around to organizing them. This was because they never had the patience to sit down and do it.

- **They may interrupt or make "off the wall" comments.**

Many ADD adults are accused of being rude because they interrupt people in the middle of a sentence. What people don't understand is, that when this ADD adult has an idea or comment to make, they will forget it if they wait too long. Therefore, they may interrupt. Others interpret this as rudeness, and it is. However, the ADD adult has trouble controlling themselves.

Ironically, some ADD adults are just the opposite. Because they recognize that they are prone to interrupt, they say nothing at all. They avoid embarrassment by keeping quiet.

· **They react strongly to bad news.**

Remember, ADD adults, because of the chemical imbalance, often have stronger emotions than others. Therefore, when something negative occurs, their reaction is likely to be strong. They may blow up and say things that are insulting to those around them. They may blame certain people and make threats. The next day, after they have calmed down, they may act as if nothing occurred. This is because they may not be aware of their over-reaction and how it affected those around them. They have done this all of their life so they see nothing abnormal about their behavior. They don't understand why others make such a big deal about their "past" behavior. Those who work around them may be confused by their reactions.

· **Some like variety and some like rigid schedules.**

This may sound contradictory but opposite extremes are common among those who have ADD.

Please note that I said extremes. Those who like rigid schedules are trying to compensate for their inability to be organized. They recognize that if they don't stick to a rigid way of doing things, they may not function well. Constantly making adjustments in an unstructured or unfamiliar situation is difficult for the ADD adult.

Those on the opposite extreme, like variety. They are basically "going along with" their internal need to keep doing things in order to work off energy. It also allows them to avoid boredom. (One of the aforementioned is not necessarily better than the other. Everyone is different, even those with ADD. What works for one may not work for another.)

- **They have trouble listening to long and complicated explanations or directions.**

These directions or explanations may have to be explained in several different ways and often. If they aren't, the ADD adult may not follow through.

The basic problem is that they have trouble concentrating for long periods of time. This is why things must be broken down into smaller pieces. They are more likely to pay attention to short directives. This requires the individual giving these directives to be part "psychologist". They have to figure out a way to break things apart and present them in an understandable manner.

As you can see, employers are more likely to hire someone who doesn't have these problems. It requires too much time to explain things in detail to an ADD adult. Therefore, employers may fire them and hire someone who learns faster.

This is an example of why an ADD adult should take medication for this disorder. The medication may enable them to understand things more quickly. Thus, being treated with medication may allow them to maintain their job.

SPECIFIC OCCUPATIONS

Based on my experience, I have noticed a trend in occupational preferences of ADD adults.

Do not assume that the following list is complete and that these are the only occupations of ADD adults. They work in all fields but I have seen a large number in the following areas.

- **Military**

I feel there are a large number of ADD adults in the military because of the structure, job security, and the constant possibility of excitement and frequent moves. The reason I feel that there are a lot of ADD adults in the military is because of the large number of ADD children who are military dependents. I have seen many military dependents who had ADD. This may be coincidental because military people have good insurance coverage. This may have allowed them to seek help more often than the average person.

However, in my work with schools, I have noticed that the elementary schools close to military bases, have a large percentage of ADD children.

- **Police Officer or Security Guard**

This is closely related to the military. The job security, possibility of excitement, and ability to move about freely as a person in authority is one of the attractions of this type of occupation.

As strange as it may sound, jobs that involve wearing a uniform is appealing to the ADD adult.

Wearing a uniform reduces the decision making process. They don't have to decide what kind of clothing to wear each day.

I've seen many ADD adults who were in the military. When these adults wore civilian clothing (especially men), they looked rather odd. They seemed to have no concept of how to coordinate their shirts, pants, socks, and shoes.

(This is similar to Add children. Parents have noted that their ADD child has a difficult time making decisions, especially about clothing. What they do choose to wear, is often unusual.)

- **Skilled Trades**

This is a broad category. The common denominator in this category is the use of their hands in putting things together. Mechanics are one of the more common jobs to which ADD adults gravitate.

This type of job allows them to work with their hands and work alone. It also allows them to avoid a great deal of paperwork.

- **Truck Driver**

This type of job fits those who are more restless and need to be on the go. Some ADD adults need very little sleep, therefore they are ideal for long distance hauling jobs. (Ironically, truck drivers' sometimes are known to use "Bennies". This is short for Benezidrine. This is one of the medications used for ADD.)

• **Creative Skills**

This is not so much of an occupation as it is a description of a skill that many ADD adults have. They may be talented in the arts (ie., music, poetry, or drawing).

I've encountered a large number of extremely talented musicians who had ADD. They learned how to play piano or other instruments quickly. The problem was, they didn't have the patience to practice. Therefore, they never took advantage of their abilities.

I had a client who was the road manager of a famous rock group (I won't mention their name). He agreed that a large number of people with whom he associated, had children who had ADD or exhibited the classic traits themselves. He also shared his view that the long hours required to do road trips would be very difficult for those who did not have a great deal of energy.

There are several movie stars that have ADD. Because ADD adults have strong emotions, it is easy to see how acting would fit them well.

Even as children, they are often overly dramatic or quick witted and funny. This quick wit was often developed as a defense mechanism to avoid facing their deficiencies. Many became class clowns because the school work was "boring". It was boring because it was hard.

They diverted attention from their deficiencies by being funny or disruptive. This was less embarrassing than admitting their problems with learning.

Numerous movie stars have ADD, but they are often anti-ADD and medication. They like to focus on how they overcame obstacles. They give their <u>philosophy</u> of life and make pseudo-intellectual statements such as: "Don't give up on your dream, just keep trying. If you want it badly enough, you can achieve it".

They know absolutely <u>nothing</u> about the number of ADD adults who have suffered severe problems. Unfortunately, these stars influence others into falsely thinking that "trying harder" is the key. They are wrong. Some ADD adults try as hard as they can, but still have severe problems. I'm only <u>guessing</u>, but I feel that one of Hollywood's most famous actor/comedians has ADD (possibly with hyperactivity). He almost <u>never</u> stops joking. He is constantly bombarded with ideas and thoughts. He switches from topic to topic and can talk incessantly. He's funny, but admits that he doesn't understand how he does this. He recently had a child. Based on his comments, this child is very active and difficult to parent. I'm sure this star would be insulted if I told him that he and his child should be treated for ADD (or at least tested). However, there is a very good chance that his child is going to have problems at some point. This may change his mind.

In summary, I will say that our economy ... the competence of our work force ... is adversely effected by the untreated ADD adults in our society.

Letter

Dear Mr. Hunsucker,

I am a 44 year old man, married with two children.

I recently learned of ADD from my sister-in-law, whose first born son has been diagnosed as having ADD.

In reading parts of your book, I feel that I too have ADD. On page 13 of your book, I read the list of symptoms of ADD and can remember that almost all of these applied to myself when I was in school (grade school, high school, college, art school, and the military).

I am fairly certain that my 15 year old son also has ADD. I feel a ray of light has come into my wife's and my life with regards to my son's educational problems.

The reason, however, that I am writing you is to ask you what can be done for an adult of my age. At one time in my life, I was tested as having an I.Q. between 125 and 130 but have not been able to stay in school to earn a degree. I have almost always felt that I have worked below my capabilities, but due to the fact that my basic education was so poor, I felt that I couldn't learn more complex subjects.

Sometimes I feel like I am caught up in a whirlpool and cannot get out; I don't have the basic knowledge to help myself through school. If I did go, I wouldn't be able to finish. My lack of self esteem doesn't lend itself to my looking for jobs with greater responsibilities because I am afraid that I won't be able to perform and will subsequently fail and lose the job.

Even though I feel that there is hope for me, I am feeling despair that it may slip through my fingers for lack of financial resources.

I would greatly appreciate anything that you can do for me.

I am hoping to hear from you soon although I realize that you must be a busy person and surely receiving a lot of correspondence such as mine. Thank you.

Ken

Author's Response

This letter shows the emotional and psychological impact ADD can have on a person. I can't definitely say that this person has ADD, but these are common occurrences among ADD adults. They have experienced failure so often that they no longer look for positions of greater responsibility because they are unable to take the pressure or fulfill the duties.

He mentioned that he was afraid he wouldn't be able to get help because of the cost. Actually, the cost of testing and treatment is relatively cheap.

The testing shouldn't cost more than $200-$500. The medication will cost about $500-$600 per year. (or about $40.00 per month). For the positive changes it can cause, this is the best investment he could make. It could also allow him to get a better position which pays more.

The benefits of treatment can be both financial and emotional. Financially, the benefits can be measured in money. Emotionally, there is no dollar amount that can equal the improvements in quality of life.

CHAPTER 9

ALCOHOL / DRUG ABUSE

Research clearly shows that untreated ADD adults are more likely to become involved in alcohol or drug abuse than the average population.

What I'm going to do is what research doesn't. I'm going to state why they are prone to abuse alcohol and drugs. Research only states the findings. It never goes on to explain why.

I will base my views on the background of hundreds of adults with whom I've worked, as well as the research articles listed in the back of my book. I will also rely on pure common sense and logic.

The first thing we must remember is that we are talking about ADD adults who have never been treated. This is an important point.

Before telling you why they are prone to abuse drugs and alcohol, I must explain some things about ADD that many people, especially professionals, don't seem to understand. Most professionals seem to think that ADD only affects a person's ability to perform academically.

The reason they think this, is because academic problems are measurable and, therefore, more evident. ADD also affects a person's thinking. This is important in understanding the connection between ADD and alcohol/drug usage.

To state it as simply as possible, those who have ADD have confused thinking.

To explain further, not everyone has the same degree of confused thinking, nor do they display it at all times. They work hard just to cope with daily life. Another way of saying this, is that it takes them longer to make good decisions or judgements than others.

Now I will tell you why I think that untreated ADD adults abuse alcohol or drugs. Very simply, they use alcohol or drugs as medication for their ADD. It is their treatment.

Not every untreated ADD adult is involved in alcohol or drug abuse. However, here is the manner in which many ADD people get started.

First, let us imagine that a fourteen year old boy has had ADD all of his life but has never been treated. By the time he reaches this age, he has probably experienced a great deal of negativism in his life. He is probably not doing well at home, at school, or in social relationships. He probably doesn't feel good about himself.

At the age of fourteen or fifteen, many teenagers experiment with some form of alcohol or other drug. However, if an ADD teen experiments with alcohol or drugs, it may have a different effect on them than it does other teens. They have a chemical imbalance. The alcohol/drugs may "treat" the ADD and make them feel more clear headed than they have ever felt in their life. It will now be difficult for anyone to convince this person that alcohol/drugs are bad. They actually feel better when they drink or take drugs. Because this is the wrong medication for ADD, they may become immune to it. This means that they have to increase the dose or go to stronger drugs in order to recapture that good feeling.

I have had numerous teenagers and adults report this very thing. When they drank, they felt better and could concentrate. Of the ADD adults I interviewed, many abused drugs. It was interesting to note that the favorite drug of abuse was speed. Speed is very similar to Ritalin or Dexedrine. (These are two of the medications used to treat ADD).

One teenager told me that the first time he used speed, it made him feel much different than he was told. His friends told him it would make him feel high and pep him up. When he took it, it calmed him down and allowed him to concentrate. He stated that it made him feel "normal".

A person who has ADD and takes speed, is likely to feel this way. "Speed" has a paradoxical effect on people with ADD. In other words, instead of speeding them up, it allows them to concentrate, focus, and think clearly.

I find it more than coincidental that illegal amphetamine usage (speed) is on the increase. I feel that this increase is, in part, due to the professional community not understanding ADD, or treating it properly.

It is going to be hard to convince some of those using speed that it is not good for them. If they have ADD, it is probably helping them to some extent. The unfortunate thing is, we do not know what dose they use or the quality of the speed. They probably mix it with alcohol or other drugs which may cause some negative side effects.

What these people need to know is, that if they have ADD and are properly medicated, they might be able to avoid the negative side effects of the drugs they currently use as treatment. More importantly, they may be able to concentrate, not have mood swings and function normally without abusing drugs.

Here is a quick summary of how I think ADD progresses to alcohol / drug abuse:

Person is born with ADD.
↓
They are never diagnosed or treated (those who were being treated, are taken off at an early age).
↓
They experience confused thinking and strong emotions due to the symptoms of ADD.
↓
At age 15 or 16, they experiment with alcohol/drugs.
↓
The alcohol/drugs work as medication and treats the ADD.
↓
Their thinking is less confused and they feel better emotionally.
↓
It will now be difficult to convince this person that drugs/alcohol are bad.
↓

Because of the positive effects, even if only short-lived, they may continue to use alcohol/drugs to recapture these good feelings.

↓

They have to increase the amount because their body becomes used to it.

↓

This leads to a constant pattern of using alcohol/drugs as "treatment" for ADD.

↓

They start having other problems, physically or emotionally, and try to stop.

↓

They can't stop because they have become physically and emotionally addicted.

↓

On top of this addiction, the symptoms of ADD return when they quit "treating" themselves. This intensifies the aforementioned problems.

↓

The alcohol/drug abuse and associated problems now become the focus of treatment. The real cause, ADD, is never seen or treated.

↓

They are sent to an alcohol/drug rehab program.

↓

Most of these treatment centers are against any kind of medication.

↓

Since this person has ADD (a chemical imbalance), they need to be treated with medication (the only effective treatment).

↓

They will not receive the proper treatment.

↓

The chances of them returning to alcohol/drug abuse is high.

Obviously not everyone who uses drugs has ADD. However, you must remember that drug abusers are a special population. ADD represents a higher percentage of this group than that of the average population. I would estimate it to be at least 30% to 40%. Perhaps even higher.

FINAL NOTE OF INTEREST

Society has been misled into believing that Ritalin "causes" alcohol or drug abuse. The evidence to support this rumor is <u>very convincing</u>. I will end this chapter with a quick summary, showing how those who are anti-ADD and medication, <u>manipulate</u> research findings:

Child has ADD.

↓

They are prescribed Ritalin at age 6 or 7.

↓

When they reach puberty (13 or 14), the Ritalin is no longer prescribed.

↓

They still have ADD, but are no longer being treated.

↓

The symptoms of ADD return (i.e. unclear thinking, inability to concentrate, etc.).

↓

In the teen years, they start using alcohol/drugs.

↓

It treats their ADD, and they feel better.

↓

They end up using alcohol/drugs as treatment.

↓

They are now abusing alcohol/drugs as an adult and no one sees the connection with ADD.

People who are anti-medication, point out the use of Ritalin at age 6, and then point out the alcohol/drug abuse of this individual in adulthood. They now say: "<u>Ritalin</u> leads to alcohol/drug abuse". This seems to make sense, but no one has asked the most important question: "<u>Why</u> were they placed on Ritalin in the first place?"

The answer is: They had a chemical imbalance (ADD) that needed treatment.

Letter # 1

Dear Mr. Hunsucker,

I am reading your book, Attention Deficit Disorder because the man I live with is an alcoholic. Because of the characteristics of ADD (as described to me by a friend who has adopted a child with ADD), I could see this disorder as a contributing factor to my friend's alcohol addiction. So when I read the portion of chapter one where you state treatment of ADD at an early age would reduce the crime rate, drop out rate and alcohol and drug abuse, I couldn't agree more.

The fields of psychology and medicine have always fascinated me, but in neither am I formally educated. So my agreement with your theory may not count for much. But I thought you might appreciate knowing that someone else can see your point of view. I'm anxious to continue reading your book to learn what we can do for an adult who probably has ADD that was neither diagnosed nor treated.

Since I have only read to page four so far, I've a long way yet to go. But I will continue to update this letter as I proceed.

I've finished your book, I'm glad you wrote it. I'm glad I read it.

I'm anxious to read your book on adults. I'm wondering how to suggest to my friend to seek out professional help for something such as this. He's in his thirties and may not agree that he is affected by ADD, and even if he does take it, he may not recognize a change in himself if medication does help. So what is to keep him from stopping any medication prescribed?

I wish we could get more information about his childhood from his mother. She's reluctant to discuss anything about his natural father, whom he never knew. She does say that Mike was a "loner" and that he wasn't really a bad boy - "he just had a temper and used to fight a lot".

If you can offer any suggestions I would be grateful. I love Mike dearly, but sometimes he's very difficult to live with.

Sincerely,

Kari

Author's Response

Please note that she said that she is not formally educated in the field of psychology but from reading my first book, she felt her boyfriend had the symptoms of ADD.

I write my books for the lay-person because they are the ones who need to know about ADD. They are more likely to recognize the symptoms than the professionals. This is because they see things the professionals don't. A Doctor may only spend 10-20 minutes with a person. Because this person is nervous and not in a relaxed setting, their behavior may be modified. Therefore, the Doctor may make a false diagnosis based on this short interaction.

She also mentioned that if he was treated, he may not recognize a change in himself and might stop the medication. This is true. There are no assurances of a person staying on their medication or recognizing that it is helping. It's usually the people around them that can tell the difference.

The cold hard facts are, that the older a person gets, the harder it is to turn them around. This is because they have developed habits that they don't want to change.

In relationship to the medication, I've discovered that even when a person recognizes improvements, they may eventually forget. This is because they don't see the connection between the improvements and the medication. The changes are often subtle and not immediately observable in some people.

This is why the person needs to make follow up visits with a professional who is knowledgeable about ADD. Two or three times a year is adequate, unless there are more severe problems. These sessions should be directed at reminding the person of the purpose of the medication, and how ADD causes problems if they don't take it.

Letter #2

Dear Mr. Hunsucker,

I have just finished reading a copy of your book Attention Deficit Disorder.

I am convinced as I have read this book that this is definitely a long overlooked problem. I was reminded of a Bible scripture by a statement in your Final Comment section where you stated, "lack of knowledge is the key factor". It is Hosea 4:6 "My people are destroyed for lack of knowledge." In another translation it reads, "my children perish for lack of knowledge."

My son's teachers believe that he may display certain attributes characteristic of ADD, although their knowledge of the disorder is limited. I am quite sure, however, after reading your book that my husband not only had an extreme case of ADD as a child but may continue to display some symptoms as an adult. As I read I felt I was reading a history of my husband's elementary school years and adolescent years as recounted to me by himself and most of his family.

Unfortunately, there was never any treatment and he suffers emotionally to this day from much emotional abuse through life by being called stupid, ignorant, told he could never do anything by family, friends, and teachers. I don't know if it is directly related or not but, his mother has had extensive counseling and psychiatric care including shock treatment and chemical therapy for years. According to your book this could be from not knowing how to cope with this. I believe her diagnosis has been that of Schizophrenic, so she may have had some problems herself, that were compounded by having at least one ADD child (there are 2 siblings).

It would appear my husband was the classic case, always an underachiever academically in school, he was a loner and dropped out of high school. He was a drug abuser through the latter years of his adolescence. He joined the military where he punched out his officer and received a discharge. Upon being sent home, he commenced his previous behavior as a drug abuser and was sent to a drug rehabilitation program by his parents. He got out of the hospital and began to pursue a technical degree, while still doing drugs intermittently but not as a heavy user.

The course of his life changed during this time and he became a "born-again" Christian believer (having been raised in a virtually atheist or agnostic home). His new found faith in God seemed to give him a new sense of motivation and direction. I met John later at a bible college. He excelled in his studies there but did not work. I on the other hand worked almost full time and studied). He became somewhat of a leader in prayer groups and study classes. I attribute his ability to excel, to the new found motivation in his relationship with the Lord.

We graduated from Bible college in 1984 and were married that summer. He pursued his bachelors degree and finished successfully with average grades in 1988. I have seen a direct correlation in what I would term ADD like behavior during times when he is not as active with the Lord or is disappointed in his spiritual walk. During the time when he is actively seeking the Lord he seems to have more direction and motivation. Throughout our marriage to this point there has, in my opinion, been some problem with work and employment history (he had virtually no job experience when we met due to lay offs, firings, and quitting).

Although his pursuit of spiritual things would remain active I often pushed him to be sure he did what he should and acted more like a mother at times and became quite a good nagger. This in turn would activate his temper which I was quite surprised to see could become violent, although never physically abusive. During times of depression he may threaten to have a car wreck, etc. His father mentioned his impulsiveness and over a year ago said his mother's psychiatrist believed he may have a chemical imbalance. They requested that we go to see his mother's doctor but nothing ever came of it. Her psychiatrist thought it may give some insight on her problem, and John's dad finally was ready to admit there may have been a chemical imbalance causing John's impulsiveness.

We have moved several times in our marriage and during times when he was "not doing as good spiritually" made some pretty impulsive and stupid decisions. He is now 30 years old with no work history other then theological (the church he works for is small and can not support us financially at this time).

We moved to allow him to pursue auto body at college so he would have a trade to supplement lay ministry activities, but after working at a body shop for four months he decided he didn't like it anymore. So I am working and am now possibly dealing with a child who may have ADD and a husband who was never treated and is prone to self-pity and a bad self-image if he is not doing "good Spiritually". I hope you can understand that I refer to these times of doing "good" or "bad" spiritually because I believe, as a Christian also, that when he is in good relationship with God then he has more directed motivation. When he is "out of fellowship" so to speak (i.e. not actively praying, reading his bible, fellowshipping with other believers,) he is prone to some of the ADD tendencies as described in your Book.

I attribute the fact that we are still together after six years to our Christian meeting and the fact that most of the Christian circles we are in, frown on divorce. I believe the Lord has given extra patience when necessary although threats to break up have been made.

My husband has displayed some resistance to coming for help even though I forced him to read part of your book last night. He has a basic distrust of doctors after his previous time in therapy, and having seen all of the treatment his mother has been through since he was a teenager.

Once again, thank you for your time, and thank you for writing the book. May it enlighten many.

Sincerely,

Tina

P.S. You mentioned in your last paragraph that as the reader we should become more involved. I am interested in doing so and only ask how?

Author's Response

This letter points out that her husband has been able to keep out of trouble primarily because of his strong religious faith. I believe this is true.

However, I want people to understand that even with strong religious convictions, the symptoms of a chemical imbalance (ADD) still remain. His wife points this out.

The reason I'm mentioning this is because I don't want people thinking that you can cure ADD (a chemical imbalance) through religion. Having faith in God can definitely have a positive effect on a person and it is recommended. However, it will not cure ADD.

God gave us a brain so that we could use it to solve problems like ADD. In other words, ADD and it's symptoms (ie: inability to concentrate, poor decision making) are not due to a lack of morals or faith. I don't want those who have ADD to feel guilty. It is not their fault that they inherited ADD. There are thousands of ADD adults, children, and teenagers who have a strong faith in God. However, some still end up in prison, alcoholic, or dead, as a result of not being treated properly.

She also mentioned a problem that has kept many ADD adults from seeking treatment. This was his past experiences with psychologists and counselors. I have seen this often. Because most of the professional community doesn't understand ADD, he probably spent most of his time talking to therapists and counselors. Some were probably confrontational, some just talked about every day matters, some talked about feelings and some may have tried to make him feel guilty about his actions in order to get him to improve.

In essence, he never saw how any of these people helped. If he had ADD, he was right. They were "barking up the wrong tree". The real reason that he had trouble controlling his temper and behavior was due to the symptoms of ADD. If he had been referred for medication, he may have seen a ray of hope because he would have experienced improvement.

Our Mental Health profession has to wake up. I feel that a large percentage of the people who go to therapists have ADD.

Strangely enough, this is the last thing a therapist looks for, if they look for it at all. They are too concerned with the immediate and obvious problems that are easily seen. (ie: alcohol abuse, bad temper, etc.). They seem to have absolutely no clue as to how ADD could cause these problems.

CHAPTER 10

CRIME

Research shows that those who have untreated ADD have a higher probability of ending up in prison than the average person.

I feel that our prisons are packed with people who have ADD. Not only do they have ADD, but they were never diagnosed or treated. In a sense, ADD was indirectly responsible for these people being in prison.

I write books that are not totally based on research findings because some of the things I state cannot be confirmed or denied by research at this point in time.

What I mean by this is: we can never determine just how many people in prison have ADD because they were never tested.

Even if they were tested, most would be mis-diagnosed anyway. The professionals responsible for testing don't understand ADD well enough to know how to test for it. Therefore, we can't determine exactly how many people currently in prison have ADD.

The research I referred to in the first paragraph of this chapter was based on the follow up of those <u>known</u> to have ADD. This follow up was done over a 20 year period. Based on this research, those with ADD had a higher probability of becoming imprisoned.

This research finding is extremely significant. If you will notice, this research is based on follow up studies. In other words, these people were not controlled by anyone. They had no guidelines to follow. They just lived their lives as they wanted. Some were treated with medication and some weren't. Some were treated for awhile, stopped, then started again. My point is this: both <u>treated</u> and <u>untreated</u> ADD adults were <u>included</u> in the statistics.

Do you understand what this means? This means, that even <u>with</u> the treated ADD adults included in the statistics, the findings <u>still</u> indicated a high incidence of illegal activities.

The researchers don't make a big deal of this finding. As a matter of fact, they down-play it.

I find it <u>phenomenal</u>! I ask this: what would the findings have been if <u>no one in the group had been treated?</u> I think the findings would have been even <u>more</u> astonishing.

Another important factor in this research, was the fact that these people were <u>known</u> to have ADD from an early age. This is important, because this undoubtedly helped some of these people. They <u>knew</u> they had ADD, which means they probably understood the reason for some of their behaviors. This <u>had</u> to help some of them. Perhaps they had fewer self-doubts and didn't have to search for answers.

Again, I think that the research findings would have been <u>worse</u> if <u>no one</u> had <u>known</u> they had ADD. Obviously, you can't do research like this. <u>Somebody</u> has to know. But, my point is this: there are those individuals who go through their entire lives without anyone knowing they had ADD. They have never been given an explanation as to <u>why</u> they <u>behave</u> or <u>feel</u> the way they do. They must search and wonder.

Common sense and logic tells me that these individuals would have a more difficult time coping than those who knew they had ADD.

I suggest that a different type of research be done on current inmates. I suggest that ADD testing be done on the inmates to see what percentage have ADD.

However, there is one <u>huge</u> problem with this. Most of the professionals who would do the testing, don't know how to properly test for ADD in children, much less adults. Therefore, the accuracy of the results will be questionable.

At some point in time, I will probably do this type of research. However, at the present time, my focus is on getting our society to understand the seriousness of this disorder.

The purpose of research, in any field, is to help predict future events. For example: if you watch 50 people jump off the Empire State Building and all of them end up dead, this is a "research" finding. You can predict, with a high degree of accuracy, that anyone who jumps off the Empire State Building is going to die. No one would condone this kind of research because "common sense" tells you what the results are going to be.

This is why I make the following statement about ADD research: It is _impossible_ and immoral to conduct the kind of research on ADD that is necessary.

For instance: we would first have to actually test and diagnose young people with ADD. The immoral portion of the research is that we would then have to _refuse_ to treat these individuals for the rest of their life, because we want to see how many of them end up in prison, commit suicide, or become alcohol/drug abusers,

This is the only way that we could _clearly_ determine what percentage of untreated ADD individuals end up with severe problems.

I don't believe anyone would ever condone such a study. I wouldn't. This is why many of my statements are based on personal experience and logical thinking. From personal experience with many ADD children, teens and adults, I have observed how many have trouble coping, especially those who were never treated. From these experiences, it is only logical to conclude that others who remain untreated may have similar problems.

What supports my thinking is the overwhelming number of letters I receive from all over the United States and Canada. Letter after letter states how someone was overlooked as a youngster, and as an adult, ended up having severe problems. Some ended up in prison.

Personally, I have no doubt about the problems that

ADD causes. However, I write this book to let others see how I came to this conclusion and let them decide for themselves if I make sense.

Not every untreated ADD adult ends up in prison. However, I feel that 30-40% of the people in prison have ADD. I will now state why I mention this percentage.

ADD is approximately 10% of the <u>average</u> population. Remember, the people in prison represent a <u>special</u> population. Research suggests that the number of those with ADD in this population is higher than that in the average population. As stated earlier, there is no way to know the exact percentage. Actually, I may be <u>understating</u> the numbers. What is clear, is that ADD is higher in the prison population. Even if it's only 30%, this is a lot of people.

Reasons for ADD adults becoming involved in crime is due to a variety of symptoms. Impulsiveness, strong emotional reactions, and making poor decisions and judgements are the primary ADD symptoms that lead to criminal behavior.

Impulsiveness is a common trait among those with ADD. They don't think before they act. Consequently, they do something on the spur of the moment which could lead to trouble.

ADD adults are prone to make poor decisions and judgements, which means that they will not consider the possible consequences of their actions. As children, many have poor comprehension. They are not able to put information together as quickly as others. Remember, they are able to comprehend, but they may be much slower than others. Needless to say, the speed with which you understand things makes a difference in the decisions you make.

Since ADD people are slow in synthesizing information and making decisions, they are easily influenced by other people who are more assertive. Another person may pressure them into taking action without thinking of the consequences. The ADD person gets caught up in the "emotions of the moment".

I've had numerous ADD adults tell me that their illegal acts were stupid. They only realized this after the fact. They were not thinking things through before they committed the act. They were caught up in the illogical rationalizing of their assertive accomplice. They were influenced by what the other person was saying, rather than relying upon clear, logical thinking.

Most ADD adults are intelligent. Even those in prison are not stupid. They do not have the ability to control their emotions and impulses as well as others can. Intelligence and control over emotions and impulses, are not the same thing. ADD adults who become involved in criminal activities have the intelligence but not the comprehension, emotional, or impulse control that others have.

This is not an excuse for their behavior. It is an explanation. I feel that if they commit a crime, they should pay for it; ADD or not. I want to prevent this behavior by early diagnosis and proper treatment.

Letter #1

Dear Mr. Hunsucker,

I am the mother of a 20 year old son, Marc. He has just been diagnosed with ADD. I got your book today. My son and I read it together. Then we held each other and cried - finally someone put a name on this "beast" after all these years of chaos, tears and confusion. Marc's just started on medication - the doctor is very reluctant, but we've been pretty insistent. As I've read your book, we felt like you were writing about Marc, but a few things are different, why I'm not sure. My husband and I are devout Catholics and we have been very involved in marriage encounter - our marriage relationship is strong, healthy and happy. We've leaned on each other through all of this. Neither of us use alcohol or drugs - but my husband's father is an alcoholic - 5 of his brothers were alcoholic and 2 of his mother's brothers are alcoholics. There is no drug or alcohol abuse in my family. My husband and I are both college graduates. I'm an R.N. with several years experience in working with the Mentally Retarded and a strong background in Behavior Modification.

I knew Marc was "different" by the time he was 3 months old. He already at that age threw temper tantrums. By the time he was 9 months, he was walking and talking and at 2, he threw tantrums that would last 2 hours if ignored. He was so inquisitive - but I thought it was maybe because he was so bright. When he went to school, the nightmares began. By 2nd grade, he was already "labeled". The teachers already knew about him, but he maintained A - B level work. At 5th grade, we had him evaluated at a child's psych clinic.

They said I was a rotten mother. The acting out behavior continued. He kept his grades at A - B level all through school. In Jr. High, he broke into the school, blew up a wood stove and vandalized a car and shoplifted. Our family doctor sent us to a psychiatrist. We were in family counseling for 6 months and the counselor who was working with us sent Marc to a child psychologist who evaluated Marc and told us that in 15 years of testing, Marc was one of the brightest kids he'd ever evaluated. His I.Q. was 146. He told me that Marc was just bored and his behavior was probably because he was looking for something better or more stimulating to do.

Since we were in a small school without much but Special Ed, we were told Marc just had to weather it out and when he got to college, he'd be fine. Marc graduated 5th in his class with a GPA of 3.6, got a 27 on his A.C.T.'s and landed an R.O.T.C. scholarship. He didn't act out a lot in school as long as the teachers let him read, do art work or whatever during class. He only had some academic problems if the course required studying and attention to details - like Marc's foreign languages. In the meantime, the chaos continued at home and out of class.

He wrecked nearly every car we owned, picked things up that weren't his, etc. We live in the north - he chose a college on the East Coast. With no control, everything fell apart. After 1-1/2 years, he was back home - He'd been arrested for theft, kicked out of his fraternity, and was academically 1.8 G.P.A. with the Army breathing down his neck. He transferred back here and lived at home this last semester trying to put it back together. We noticed a use - not yet abuse - of alcohol that hadn't been there before, his morals were gone and his self concept at it's worst. Living at home didn't help him academically - the G.P.A. went to 1.3 even though he appeared to be studying and trying. My husband wanted to throw him out of the house. One day in May, I was unloading on a friend of mine who's a school psychologist. He's known Marc for years. He looked kind of surprised and said, you mean Marc's never been diagnosed - I think he is pretty classic ADD. I thought you knew. I passed the information on to Marc, along with the fact that I'd shared this with our family doctor who was willing to find someone who'd work with Marc. Marc sought treatment on his own and was diagnosed without much trouble. Our family doctor's wife recommended your book - they have a son with ADD - just diagnosed a year ago - he is 7.

Marc could tell the difference immediately with medication. The first day he took it, he went to work and the errors he made on the job reduced remarkably. He's changed his major in college.

At this point I'm almost afraid to hope. We've struggled for so many years with disorganization, mood swings, inability to finish projects without someone riding his tail, impulsive behavior, aggression, and mouthiness, it seems impossible to believe that it's all due to a chemical imbalance that can be pretty much controlled with medication. I really am afraid to hope. My husband is a gentle loving man who's always put his wife and kids at the top of his priorities. He's been a scoutmaster, little league coach, teaches at church, but he's really burned out. He's got a lot of bitterness toward Marc - more than me. I yell and holler and scream when I'm at wits end, then it's over, the anger dissipates. As I read your book, I understand you to say these kids really can't help it - anymore than a diabetic can help it?? Right?? I don't want to make excuses for Marc - I just want to help him. I do have concerns about treatment - that we have a doctor who will cooperate. He diagnosed ADD, but is really reluctant to use medication. He started Marc on Meds, but directed him to only take it the days he was working. I tend to think he's not going to want to prescribe for weekends and school breaks. I'm not the least bit afraid of medication - given the alternative of having Marc drink beer - I'll take the medication.

Thank you so much for your book. I cried several times when I read it - but they're not the same kind of tears I've shed for Marc in the past 20 years. I feel like I've been groping in a dark room for 20 years and I've finally found the light switch! God bless you and thank you for your work.

Judy

Author's Response

This letter covers a lot of problem areas, and I probably can't make any comments that will be any more clear than hers. However, I once again want to point out the similarities in this letter to that of others.

- History of alcohol abuse in the family.
- Very intelligent child.
- Parents sought help but were still seen as the problem.
- Several car wrecks.
- Medication almost instantly changed him.

She mentioned that it was hard for her to believe that all of these things were due to a chemical imbalance. It isn't hard for me to believe because I've seen hundreds of children and adults change almost overnight when this chemical imbalance was treated properly (this doesn't happen every time, though).

ADD causes many problems and the professional community in the United States lacks the knowledge to diagnose and treat it. Through reading this book, I hope they will gain some knowledge.

Letter #2

I have just finished reading your book on ADD and I want to thank you from the bottom of my heart! Finally, someone understands what it is like to fight daily with concentration on everything one does. Tears came to my eyes, because someone accepted what I have felt for some 40 years. I have heard all the labels used that professionals and others conjure up as the cause of my deficiency and still hear them describing my children.

In 40 years, the lack of compassion or understanding has not changed. Not only has it been extremely frustrating for me, but painful, also causing my feeling of never measuring up to society's expectations. However, with all these adversities in my life, despite a few mistakes, I was able to overcome many of my shortcomings. I have since had to realize that my father's very positive attitude had a major influence on my life. While I exhibited many of the same problems described in your book, I also learned to work around my deficiencies in many ways; and I was able to teach my children how to use these methods to help themselves. This was long before I knew that my three older children or myself had ADD.

Three years ago, my youngest child was exhibiting behavioral problems and a parent of a child with ADD explained the deficiency to me. My daughter was tested and diagnosed with ADHD (2) and ADD (1). I was not tested but, while my youngest child was being tested, I mentally took the test. I found I had the same problems she had! It finally made sense to me why I had so much trouble concentrating, coordination problems, memory loss, etc.

When my older son went into high school, I recognized one important thing: all of us could learn much more easily when taught visually. I put my son in a Vocational High School and he graduated and is on his way to being an electrician with a 3.7 average! My older daughter and myself learned in-depth knowledge of computers by hands-on training and my youngest son is now in Commercial Art, working for a newspaper. He graduated from a vocational college with a 4.0 average! He is the one with ADD. I firmly believe that my ex-husband has ADD too. He was also adopted. I'm not sure how we managed to hold a marriage together for as long as we did.

I now work for the State Prison. The ironic part is that eight out of the eleven inmates that I recommended for testing proved to have ADD. It's so strange, but after a few days of knowing an inmate, I seem to be able to pick out the ones with ADD. It's almost as if I recognize it! This probably sounds absurd, but for some reason these people stand out to me.

Sincerely,

Jane

Author's Response

If you can read between the lines, you can see the emotional impact that just reading about ADD had on this person. She felt that someone understood. We must remember things like this when we consider the thousands of children and adults who still don't know they have ADD.

This person is able to express herself fairly well. She was able to compensate for her problems and she noted that her father had a strong positive influence. Again, we must consider the thousands of people who were not lucky enough to have all of these influences in their life. These people are doing even worse than those who wrote these letters. However, there are many ADD adults who had positive influences in their life but they still ended up with severe problems because of the ADD.

She mentioned societies lack of compassion and understanding. This is true. Most people consider the behavior of ADD adults as nothing more than them not "choosing" to control themselves. Because society doesn't understand ADD, they don't see how it could cause problems related to behavior. ADD is not understood in children, so I can guarantee you that it is even less understood in adults.

Also note that she works in a prison and notices a lot of people who seem to have ADD. I agree. As I state in other parts of this book, I feel that ADD is the cause of a large number of people being in prison. I feel that if these people had been properly treated and diagnosed, they may not have ended up in this situation.

Chapter 11

SUICIDE

Earlier, I briefly mentioned suicide. I now feel that a more in - depth discussion is needed.

Research shows that those with ADD are more likely to commit or attempt suicide. What research doesn't explain is why? I will try to explain how ADD can lead to suicide.

The first thing I want to do is focus on the difference in the suicide rate between males and females in the United States. (I'm not just talking about those with ADD, I'm talking about the entire population.)

According to the statistics presented by the Bureau of Census, 1991, here is the difference between male and female suicide. (These figures represent the number of suicides per 100,000 population.)

WHITES:

20-24 Years of Age

Year	Males	Females	Summary
1970	19.3	5.7	3.4 x as many Males
1980	27.8	5.9	4.7 x as many Males
1988	27.0	4.4	6.1 x as many Males

25-34 Years of Age

Year	Males	Females	Summary
1970	19.9	9.0	2.1 x as many Males
1980	25.6	7.5	3.2 x as many Males
1988	27.7	6.1	4.2 x as many Males

BLACKS:

20-24 Years of Age

Year	Males	Females	Summary
1970	18.7	4.9	3.7 x as many Males
1980	20.0	3.1	6.4 x as many Males
1988	19.8	2.9	6.8 x as many Males

25-34 Years of Age

Year	Males	Females	Summary
1970	19.2	5.7	3.3 x as many Males
1980	21.8	4.1	5.3 x as many Males
1988	22.1	3.8	5.8 x as many Males

What this shows is that the suicide rate for males is between 4 and 6 times that of females.

Think about this. . . 4 to 6 times higher in males. Doesn't anyone besides me think that this is <u>unusual</u>?

Yes, I've heard what the experts have said about the difference in male and female suicide. They say that men are <u>more violent</u> in the <u>methods</u> they use (i.e. guns) therefore, they are more likely to succeed in suicide.

This is <u>not</u> an answer as to why more men kill themselves! Telling me that they use guns only <u>describes</u> the <u>method</u> they use. It doesn't explain <u>why</u> they kill themselves, or why they <u>want</u> to kill themselves.

The most widely accepted explanation for a higher suicide rate among men is how our society treats them. We teach them to not express their feelings and to be "macho". This explanation makes sense. But, let us analyze this more closely.

I might be able to accept this as an explanation for the suicide rate of men being <u>double</u> that of women. I might even be able to "stretch" my imagination and accept this as an explanation for the suicide rate to be <u>3 times</u> that of women.

However, when someone tells me men kill themselves 4 to 6 times more than females because society teaches them to be macho, I have problems accepting this. There has to be more to it.

You will notice that the gap between males and females <u>increased</u> in the last 20 years. It's going up among men and <u>down</u> among women.

If we accept the theory of the "experts", our society (in some mysterious way) must be teaching males to be even <u>less open</u> with their feelings and <u>more</u> macho.

<u>This</u> is hard to believe!

We would have to have <u>camps</u> or schools that openly <u>teach</u> men to hide their emotions and be macho to account for such a large gap.

I don't know if even <u>this</u>, would translate into such a high <u>suicide</u> rate!

I say, something is wrong with the traditional explanation, regardless of ADD. However, I think that ADD plays a part in these statistics being so lop-sided.

First, I will make a list of things you need to understand about ADD before I show how all of these items relate to the topic of suicide.

- 10 times more men have ADD than women.
- Those with ADD have had a history of failures in school, home, and in personal relations.
- Those with ADD have very strong emotional reactions to events.
- Those with ADD are impulsive and do things without considering the consequences.
- Those with ADD have more problems holding jobs and maintaining relationships.
- ADD is hereditary.
- Those with ADD have a low self-esteem.

I'm not saying that everyone who commits suicide has ADD. I'm saying that when you read the list of traits among those with ADD, you will see a list of traits that are <u>common</u> to those who are <u>more likely</u> to commit suicide.

This similarity can't be ignored or written off with some simplistic explanation usually provided by the "experts".

Here is a brief summary of the sequence of events that leads to the ADD adult's contemplation of suicide:

The ADD adult has had ADD all of his life, but has never been diagnosed or treated.
↓
He has always struggled in school and had to endure more stress than others.
↓
His parents had to stay on top of him more than they did his siblings. Consequently, he received more negative feedback from his parents than most kids.
↓
Because of his "immature" and impulsive behaviors, he has few friends and trouble maintaining relationships (especially with females). The friends he does have are similar to him.
↓
After high school, if he finishes, he is unable to maintain a job for any length of time.
↓
He abuses alcohol or other drugs.
↓
He may recognize that his life is in a mess and try to change.
↓

He is unable to change as quickly as he would like because he is battling a chemical imbalance and he doesn't know it.

↓

He may sink into depression because of the accumulative affect of his negative life experiences.

↓

This depression is compounded by the chemical imbalance. (He feels his depression more strongly than others)

↓

Because of his unclear thinking (the results of ADD), he sees no future or hope.

↓

He may sense that he needs to live for the moment because intuitively, he feels he has nothing to lose.

↓

He may engage in risk-taking behavior or ignore the rules of society.

↓

He may have a "close call" with death through car accidents, violence, or drug abuse.

↓

When all of the aforementioned traits are combined with impulsive behaviors, you now have an individual who is at risk of attempting or committing suicide.

Everything that I have just written is based on my interviews with ADD adults who have reported these experiences. Remember, this is just an example because it is impossible to determine exactly what causes a person to commit suicide. We can't ask them, so we have to speculate as to their reason.

Suicide Among Blacks

If you will notice, the gap between men and women is consistent between blacks and whites. (The census only mentioned blacks and whites). In 1988, black males (age 20-24) had a suicide rate that was 6.8

times that of black females. This is an astounding number.

The suicide rate of black males is higher than that of white males. But, the rate of suicide for <u>black females</u> is <u>lower</u> than that of <u>white females</u>. My point is this: As a group, <u>blacks do not</u> kill themselves more often than whites. However, <u>black males do</u> kill themselves more often than <u>white males</u>.

Both black and white males have a suicide rate that fluctuates between 4 and 6 times that of females of <u>both</u> races.

What I'm trying to do, is show that <u>racism</u>, although it <u>definitely exists</u>, is not the <u>primary</u> factor in this lop-sided suicide rate. Racism does play a part, I'm sure of it, but the suicide rate of <u>black females</u> is the <u>lowest</u> among all groups. This is a statistic that is difficult to explain if someone uses the theory of racism or color.

Again, I think there is a connection between <u>ADD</u> and the extremely high suicide rate for <u>black males</u>.

To explain the connection, I must once again refer to the list mentioned earlier in this chapter. In addition to this, I must add some information about why ADD is overlooked.

Untreated ADD adults, regardless of color, have more problems coping with life. If they had been treated, there is a chance they would not have had as many problems.

Since ADD is overlooked in <u>white</u> males, I believe

that it is even more overlooked in <u>black</u> males.

There are a number of reasons for this. The most common reason is the same as it is for whites; lack of knowledge of the professionals.

However, there are some sociological reasons that ADD is overlooked in blacks. These are based on white racism, black mistrust of whites, and the lower economic status of blacks.

To summarize, I feel that since ADD is more often overlooked in black males, this means that there are more <u>untreated</u> ADD <u>black males</u> than untreated ADD white males. Therefore, more black ADD males will show up in the statistics of suicide, as well as the other <u>special populations</u> occupied by those with ADD.

My major point in writing this chapter is: untreated ADD can lead to a person taking their own life. Treatment, with medication, can dramatically reduce the chance of suicide. This is why I constantly tell people that they had better quit looking up the side effects of medication, and start focusing on ADD and what can happen if it isn't treated.

CHAPTER 12

OVERLOOKED IN CHILDHOOD MISDIAGNOSED IN ADULTHOOD

As time marches on, the person with <u>untreated</u> ADD develops other problems. These are caused by the symptoms of ADD, but no one sees the connection. They see the problem, but not the ADD. Here are some of the problems that untreated ADD adults are misdiagnosed as having:

1. Depression

2. Manic-depression

3. Anxiety disorder

4. Obsessive-compulsive disorder

5. Phobias

6. Conduct or oppositional disorder

7. Anti-social personality

8. Addictions

9. The newest ADD mis-diagnosis (Munchhausen by Proxy)

I will now give an explanation as to how and why ADD people are mis-diagnosed as having one or more of these disorders. Again, not everyone who has one of these disorders has ADD. I'm talking about people who have ADD but are mistakenly diagnosed as having one of these disorders.

DEPRESSION

It's not unusual for untreated ADD adults to be depressed. Therefore, the diagnosis of depression is partly correct. This depression is both physical and psychological, but both are caused by ADD. For instance: people with ADD feel their emotions stronger than others because of the chemical imbalance. This is the physical aspect of their feeling deeply depressed. The psychological depression is caused by the accumulation of disappointments and failures since childhood. The physical and psychological depression may combine in the following way:

Event occurs (i.e. divorce)
↓
Psychological depression occurs
↓
Chemical imbalance of ADD causes an overreaction to this feeling
↓
They now feel much more depressed than others who undergo similar events.
↓
Consequently, they are diagnosed as "Depressed".

The ironic aspect of depression and ADD is that the same medication is often used to treat both. What often happens is that an ADD person is initially treated for depression. Because they are prescribed the medication that is effective for ADD, they feel better. Unfortunately, ADD doesn't get recognized as the problem because the name of the medication, "anti-depressant," is <u>adopted</u> as the diagnosis or problem.

There are specific anti-depressants that have been proven to be effective for ADD in Adults (Tofranil and Norpramine). Other anti-depressants have been used but they are not as effective as these two. Clients comment that the other medications made them feel better and not care about their problems, but it didn't help their concentration or attention span. On the other hand, Tofranil and Norpramine helped all areas, especially the attention span and concentration.

MANIC DEPRESSION

This is very similar to depression. The chemical imbalance is what causes the person to <u>appear</u> to be manic or depressed.

Again, when an ADD person feels their emotions, they feel them <u>stronger</u> than the average person. Therefore, when they feel happy, they are on top of the world. When they are depressed, they are deeply depressed.

These moods <u>don't</u> change <u>instantly</u>. At the start of the day, a pattern may appear. One day the chemical reaction may cause a "manic", or good mood. On another day, they may become more depressed. Why? No one knows. The chemical just happens to give a different message that day.

I've had parents say this about their ADD child. They can tell in the morning, if it's going to be a good day or a bad day. The child can eat the exact same foods each day, but still be completely different from one day to the next. I mention this for those of you who are prone to think that allergies or diets are the explanation for these changes in behavior. (I talk about allergies, diet and ADD in other parts of the book.)

Adults with ADD often have manic-depressive traits. Professionals who diagnose ADD adults as manic-depressive make this mistake because they don't get enough background information. If they would investigate this adult's childhood, they would have discovered that they may have had the classic academic and behavioral problems of ADD children. As the years progressed, the other traits of ADD (i.e. strong emotional reactions to events) became more of a problem than the academic problems.

To summarize, professionals don't check an adult's background close enough to see if there has been a history of problems such as ADD that could be the cause of their current behavior.

ANXIETY DISORDER

Many people with ADD have an internal drive or need to be in constant motion. When I say in constant motion, I don't necessarily mean physically. They also keep in constant mental motion. The best example I can give is with children. Many parents are confused when they are told their child has ADD. They think that ADD means the same thing as hyperactive. Therefore, they say, "My child isn't hyper, he can sit for hours and play video games."

What they don't understand is that video games

provide a great deal of <u>mental activity</u>. They are <u>constantly</u> thinking and staying busy. This is the equivalent to the child who is in constant motion in the classroom.

ADD adults have a low frustration tolerance. Therefore, they are prone to anxiety, more so than the average person. To summarize this section; ADD adults are <u>very</u> likely to have the symptoms of an <u>anxiety disorder</u>.

OBSESSIVE-COMPULSIVE DISORDER

It's hard for people to understand how a person with ADD can be obsessive-compulsive. Most ADD people are known to be disorganized (in both their thinking and physical environment). This is totally opposite from the obsessive - compulsive person. Obsessive - compulsive people are usually overly organized and perform the same action or have the same thought repeatedly.

Here is how an ADD person becomes obsessive - compulsive.

Because they are disorganized, they develop a method of compensating for this disorganization. Unfortunately, they may over-compensate by becoming extremely organized and very rigid. It seems that they <u>intuitively</u> recognize that they have a problem with organization. Therefore, they have a place for everything.

Many ADD people have a bad memory. Consequently, they've learned to check everything several times to make sure they haven't overlooked anything. This is especially true when leaving the house. They may check the stove, locks, and furnace several times before leaving. They also make lists for everything.

As you can see, any professional who observes this behavior could easily <u>mis-interpret</u> it as obsessive - compulsive.

PHOBIAS

Phobias are caused by an excessive amount of anxiety about certain items or situations.

It's not unusual for ADD people to have a variety of fears, even in childhood. One of the most common among children is "school phobia." Many people laugh when they hear this term. They think of a child who resists going to school. A school phobic is much more than this.

I have seen teenagers screaming, crying, and with expressions of terror on their face when parents or others "forced" them to go to school. These adults didn't believe this child truly had a phobia until they actually witnessed the child's reaction.

The reason school phobias occur among ADD children is rather obvious. They have academic problems due to the symptoms of ADD. This leads to a great deal of anxiety. Eventually, they attach this feeling to the environment in which the fear occurs. They may not feel the anxiety on weekends, during the summer, at church, or at other gatherings; only when in or near a school building. Their brain has to have some explanation as to why they are experiencing this anxiety. Since there is no <u>logical</u> explanation, an illogical explanation is sufficient. The brain tells them that "<u>somehow</u>", being near a school is dangerous. Obviously, this is on a subconscious level because most of the time, they can tell you that it's <u>stupid</u> to be afraid of a school building. Even with this <u>conscious</u> knowledge, they still become extremely scared when near a school.

Another phobic response I've witnessed in children is called <u>separation anxiety</u>. This is when the child has trouble being away from a parent, usually the mother, for a long period of time. They have the fear that the parent will either die or just disappear. Remember, those with ADD feel their emotions stronger than others. Therefore, if an event caused this person to suspect that the parent may die (i.e. the parent may have had to be hospitalized for a period of time), then their reaction to this event may be more severe than the non-ADD child. This makes them more prone to have a separation anxiety than the non-ADD child.

Needless to say, the type of phobia an ADD adult acquires is dependent upon their experiences. I would like to say that everyone who has a phobia does not necessarily have ADD. I'm merely pointing out <u>how those who have ADD</u>, may develop phobias.

CONDUCT OR OPPOSITIONAL DISORDER

These two are closely related. The only difference is that one (oppositional) is not as severe as the other (conduct). Oppositional disorder usually refers to children and conduct disorder often refers to teenagers.

Most ADD teens who have behavior problems are diagnosed as conduct disorder. Unfortunately, no one even knows they have ADD. If they are known to have ADD, most professionals don't understand how it has anything at all to do with behavior. Consequently, ADD is ignored and everyone begins treating the "symptom" . . . bad behavior.

The juvenile probation departments throughout the nation have thousands of ADD teenagers who are mis-diagnosed as conduct disorders. This mis-diagnosis is extremely important to all of us because their treatment, is based on their diagnosis. In other words, hundreds of thousands of ADD teens are sent for the wrong treatment. This costs us, the taxpayers, millions of dollars because the treatment isn't successful. These teens continue to get into trouble. The lives of many of these teenagers are ruined because they have been mis-diagnosed and mis-treated.

ANTI-SOCIAL PERSONALITY DISORDER

Some of those who had a conduct disorder or oppositional disorder as youngsters develop into anti-social personalities as adults. This isn't always the case. Not everyone who has a conduct or oppositional disorder becomes anti-social.

However, anyone who has an anti-social personality disorder probably had a conduct or oppositional disorder in childhood. In other words, there is usually a childhood history of behavior problems in the adult with an anti-social personality.

As stated earlier, those with ADD often have a conduct or oppositional disorder. If they remain untreated for 20-30 years, the odds increase that they will become anti-social personalities. Unfortunately, these adults are often diagnosed as anti-social but the true cause, ADD, was never diagnosed or treated. Therefore, only their current behavior is focused upon. If they had been properly treated for ADD <u>as a child</u>, they may not have developed into anti-social adults.

ADDICTIONS

Research shows that untreated ADD adults are more prone to become involved in addictive behaviors than the average population. Therefore, you will find a high percentage of ADD adults among alcohol/drug abusers. Another addictive behavior that is common to ADD individuals is cigarette smoking. They may also use a great deal of caffeine.

The explanations for the ADD person becoming involved in any of these addictive behaviors is simple. The substances they become addicted to actually <u>treats</u> their chemical imbalance. They initially start using a substance because it makes them <u>feel</u> better, think more clearly, or calms them down. The longer they use it, the more they need. Because their body builds up a tolerance, eventually they have to use an excessive amount of the substance to receive minimal benefits. Other parts of their body may now become adversely affected by this substance. They may develop a <u>physical</u> need to maintain a certain level of this substance in their blood stream. It will now be difficult for them to stop using it, even when they want to.

If the ADD person had been treated with the proper medication at an early age, the chances of them using other substances as their <u>treatment</u>, would have been substantially reduced.

Once a person has an addiction, most professionals focus on stopping the addiction instead of discovering what might have been the cause.

Again, ADD adults often have the symptoms of the aforementioned disorders. Therefore, these diagnoses are partly correct. What is incorrect is the professional's judgement as to the cause of a particular diagnosis. It's extremely important that the correct cause of the disorder is found. The cause will determine the treatment to be used.

For example: If the cause of a person's depression is a chemical imbalance such as ADD, then the use of medication on a long term basis is the proper treatment. If the cause is psychological, then counseling will be the proper treatment. (What I mean by psychological is when a person experiences depression because of some event such as the death of a family member).

What I've discovered, is that most professionals immediately assume that the cause is psychological. This has led to the improper treatment of thousands of ADD adults.

THE NEWEST ADD MIS-DIAGNOSIS

Note: I foresee a new method of mis-diagnosing or overlooking ADD. It's called, "Munchhausen by Proxy." This is not a true diagnostic category. It is not recognized by the American Psychiatric Association.

In fact, the true diagnostic category is called Facetious disorder. This is recognized by the American Psychiatric Association. The traits of Facetious Disorder are as follows:

A person pretends to be sick in order to receive attention. They may purposely take substances that cause certain symptoms. They enjoy "fooling" doctors and receiving attention. This disorder is sometimes referred to as <u>Munchhausen Syndrome</u>.

Now I will explain the newest "invention". It is called Munchhausen <u>by proxy</u>.

The key words are "by proxy."

Munchhausen by proxy is when a parent makes their child ill in order to receive attention. They want to be seen as good parents so they rush the child to the emergency room. An example is when a parent holds the child's breath until they pass out. They then claim they don't know what is wrong with the child. This is a <u>very rare</u> problem, but it's receiving a great deal of media attention.

The reason I mention this "<u>syndrome</u>" in relationship to ADD is as follows:

One mother was placed in prison for child abuse, and was told she had munchhausens by proxy. She refused to agree that she had it.

She was accused of child abuse, primarily because her child had to visit the emergency room 10 or 15 times in 3 years. The doctors assumed that the mother must be doing something to the child, because it was seen as <u>impossible</u> for a child to have so many accidents or problems in one year.

Here is the problem: I have seen ADD children who have been sent to the Emergency Room <u>10 - 15</u> times in <u>one</u> year. Why? Because they are reckless, have a high tolerance for pain, and are difficult for the parent to monitor.

These parents have been reported for child abuse, for the same reason mentioned previously. No one believes the child did this by himself. However, the child <u>did</u> achieve this alone. I've seen it time and time again.

To summarize my point: I feel that <u>munchhausen by proxy</u> will be used against parents who have ADD children. Because professionals don't understand ADD, they don't understand how accident prone these children can be.

Professionals claim that these people don't <u>even know they have this "Syndrome"</u>. This is <u>Fabulous</u> for the fields of psychology and medicine. This is the ultimate <u>"cover"</u> for professionals. Although it is admitted to be <u>rare</u>, I predict it will be used a great deal in the future. Why? Because it's exactly what professionals have been looking for. They don't have to prove <u>anything</u>. They can hide behind the cloak of <u>mysticism</u>.

I just thought I would mention this "syndrome". It's not a psychological condition, it's more of a <u>legal</u> description.

I'm sure that books will explode on the scene with the "new discovery" while ADD, which is <u>very</u> common remains obscure. The media loves "new discoveries". T.V. networks will fill their schedule with anything new and different.

Letter #1

Dear Glenn,

After reading your book on ADD, I felt like the "scales had been removed from my eyes" and I suddenly understood all our struggles with our 15 and 13 year old sons. This understanding, although welcomed, brought with it grieving--grieving for myself who was brought to a Children's Hospital for several weeks when a child because I was always in motion, always dropping things and "could never do anything right." I am grieving for my younger brother who dropped out of high school, had tremendous interpersonal problems and finally, at the age of 44 when struggling to get through law school got diagnosed as ADD. When put on medicine, he found law school a breeze.

I'm grieving for my children -- that we had our older son tested by a psychologist, attended a learning center, had a tutor, went to private school, had constant help from his parents, etc. and we never knew his problem might be ADD. We endured stares from other parents and anger from team coaches over our younger son who would smart mouth them and argue back at authority, and on and on and on. I am sure you have heard plenty of stories.

I had read several books on ADD last year but came away not being sure they were describing our children. I knew my brother and a nephew back in New England were on medication and there was talk they had ADD but I didn't make the connection to my children. We just kept plodding along thinking it was a behavior problem that would be corrected with better parenting.

Your book came into my life at the right time and so perfectly described our sons that I am absolutely sure that they have ADD. I can't say I was happy to realize this -- it's like learning your child has a disability -- yet it's even worse because for years we had expected them to function like everyone else although they really had one hand tied behind their back. We had recently been to see a family therapist who seemed to be at a loss in explaining the outlandish behaviors of our youngest son. We wondered if he might be a sociopath or emotionally disturbed. I didn't think these categories fit, but it wasn't until I read your book that I knew they didn't.

Now I want to learn as much as possible about ADD and to help other professionals and parents become aware. I also want to learn more about adults who had (or still have) ADD. What behaviors should I look for in myself? How do I know if I have outgrown the disorder or have adequately compensated? Should I try medicine?

I plan to order about 50 copies of your book to mail to all we have seen regarding our children and to other pediatricians and child therapists in the area. I know the two most recommended child psychologists in this area were only looking for hyperactivity when discussing ADD -- and since my sons were not hyperactive they ruled out ADD. I think their professional judgement skewed my search.

If we had only known more sooner -- but I am grateful we know what we know now.

Thanks for listening -- and if there is any way I can help in publicizing ADD -- I want to.

Sincerely yours,

Carla

P.S.   I have my Master's Degree in Social Work and use to teach emotionally disturbed children. My husband is a medical doctor. I only mention this to highlight how long, even well educated people, can struggle in the dark without proper information. Thank you for your book. I look forward to any additional information you have prepared.

Author's Response

This letter shows how much effort, money and time the parents spent to find help for their child. They went to a variety of professionals and no one ever discussed ADD as being a possible problem, even though it is the most common reason for academic or behavior problems in children.

Notice that even though the parents kept searching for help, other people assumed it was the parents' fault that the child acted as he did. This happens often. People may even say, "you need to get that child help". Oddly enough, the parents had been trying but the professionals didn't help.

She mentions that her brother, after having problems in high school, went on to law school, after being treated with medication. This shows how quickly medication can help a person. It may only take one or two weeks to see the difference.

Again, notice how heredity plays a part. Her nephews were on medication but she didn't see any connection between them and her sons. This is because professionals don't seem to understand the heredity link. Anytime I diagnose someone as having ADD, I tell them to contact any relative who may have had academic or behavior problems and tell them to look into the possibility of ADD. Since we know it's in the family, ADD could have been the problem, but was overlooked.

Again, these are highly educated people who had no clue that ADD might be the problem. No matter how intelligent a person is, it's unlikely that they will be able to recognize ADD in themselves.

This is why I keep promoting my books on ADD. Information must consistently be put forth on ADD in order to reach people who have absolutely no understanding of ADD.

Letter #2

Dear Mr. Hunsucker,

I have recently read your book about Attention Deficit Disorder. I noted the comment in your book about writing another book concerning adults with this disorder. Have you finished the book? Where can I get a copy?

I have a child we would have never suspected to have ADD, however, we have always known that he has been "different" than his agemates. For instance, he is quite small for his age, lays awake till midnight most nights, fidgets constantly, very insecure and clingy. I always got so frustrated with him that I quit getting out the crayons and paints, stopped buying him puzzles, etc. He just couldn't do them. I would get jealous when looking at our nephew's artwork, and he is the same age. We just figured that he needed more time to mature. We sent him to private kindergarten so he could benefit from the extra attention that 2 teachers and only 14 students could provide. However, he did not excel. He barely kept up, and by the end of the year, the other students had far exceeded him in the various reading books, etc.

The first week of first grade was very upsetting for us. We received 2 calls from his teacher. Then the next week there were problems also. I called the school psychologist, and she suggested that there may be problems at home that are causing this behavior (alcoholism, divorce). This was not the case. As the end of the first month of school drew to an end, we were very concerned, and he was becoming a big problem for his teacher. (Couldn't stay in his seat, not paying attention). I decided to make an appointment with his pediatrician, and the teacher wrote me a list of his adverse behaviors, which closely match those you list in your book. The doctor said that ADD could be the case, and mentioned a double blind study using Ritalin and a placebo along with surveys. However, he recommended doing nothing except giving him extra attention at school. I took information home, explained it to his teacher, and she said that he was already getting a lot of extra attention. I worried that the teacher would lose patience with him, and stop trying to help him. I went back to the doctor and told him I wanted to do the study. We were unable to start the study for 3 weeks however, since my son, Fred, couldn't seem to remember to get the pretest survey to his teacher and then back to us. He has always had problems remembering a few directions.

We are just now starting the test, but I am positive that Fred has this disorder. The funny thing is that he's always been so pleasant to be around. He usually doesn't bounce off the walls, but he does exhibit a few of the hyperactive behaviors you mention. But for the most part, the attention deficit is the problem. From the beginning, he has been afraid of crowds and new situations. He has trouble with transitions and he was very insecure with babysitters and daycare. He was afraid to go to school, take swimming lessons, etc., because he thought I would leave and never return. I love this child and have never given him a reason to fear abandonment! We have a new tri-level home, and for the first 9 months we lived here, I had to constantly tell him where I'd be in the house. This is still the case now, but not as bad.

Here's the interesting thing. Fred's dad, my husband Jim, has had some type of mental or emotional problems ever since I've known him. We've been married 8 years now, and it has progressively gotten worse to the point where I can't stand being around him. We went to counseling that centered mostly on his mother, who has caused us a great deal of pain in our relationship. Anyway, after reading you book, and putting two and two together, I wondered if Jim could have been a child with undiagnosed ADD! I showed him the book, and talked to him and he thinks it is very likely. He is currently seeing a different doctor, and a new counselor. I've asked him to ask them about this possibility. He's going to call today. I've always felt that he is smart and has a great deal of potential inside of him, but he is unmotivated, and has low self esteem. He can't get organized, has fits of rage, sometimes acts extremely immature and he was held back in the first grade. I'm going to find out more about this from his dad. Although the doctors have not diagnosed Jim with anything, he fears that he may be schizophrenic like his mom. After reading your book, he found relief in the idea that maybe ADD is the problem!

I am anxious for your new book, to help us understand all this. I hope this is the missing piece of the puzzle we've been looking for. I'm going to go crazy if he doesn't get some help. But, help for WHAT has been the question. Now all we have to do is convince the doctors to let him try the medication. That may not be easy.

Thanks for any help in advance ...

Lisa

Author's Response

I inserted this letter because it mentions a variety of problems their ADD son has been having. I wanted you, the reader, to see a parallel between this child's problems (i.e., insecurity, fear of crowds, fear of being abandoned) and that of some adults.

When an adult has unrealistic fears, such as phobias, most professionals would never consider ADD as being the cause. However, I've seen many children, teens, and adults, who had phobia's. They had ADD since birth and they had always been fearful.

Again, most professionals lack an understanding of ADD and how it causes other disorders. When professionals deal with phobic adults, they usually assume that there is something <u>currently</u> going on in their life to cause them to be anxious. They may be right, however, they don't seem to understand that if this person has had ADD all of their life, it is probable that the ADD had something to do with this person having a phobia. Therefore, the ADD should be treated first, to see if it helps the phobia.

As I have said many times, the sequence of treatment is the key. Treat the ADD and see what it takes care of. If problems still remain, then you try other treatments. Also, note the words used by the Dr. He wanted to do a "study". Why? He should treat the child. This underlines the lack of knowledge among professionals.

CHAPTER 13

THE EVALUATION PROCESS

The evaluation process I have developed for ADD is too long and complicated to put in this book. Therefore, I only cover it in a superficial manner in order to give you, the reader, a guideline.

I've developed this evaluation process over the last 7 years (since 1986). I've added and subtracted material as I have learned more about how ADD manifests itself in an <u>observable</u> and practical manner.

The actual tests used are not complicated. What <u>is</u> complicated, is teaching an examiner how to properly administer the tests and interpret the results.

Some of the tests I administer are well known achievement, I.Q. and personality tests. The tests <u>specifically</u> for ADD, I developed. These tests are not utilized by anyone in the Nation. (I offer training and this is mentioned at the end of this chapter.)

Another important aspect of the evaluation process, is the <u>sequence</u> in which the tests are presented. The arrangement of the room, as well as the <u>behavior</u> of the examiner, is also important.

Because ADD manifests itself differently from person to person, I had to develop tests that took these differences into account (an example is the non-hyperactive person). To reduce the amount of administration time, some tests were developed in such a way as to measure several different ADD traits. This also "camouflaged" the purpose of the test.

In addition to the evaluation process, I developed 12 categories of ADD. This was done to clarify ADD and demonstrate its complexity. This also reduces the chances of an examiner coming to a false conclusion. (These 12 categories will be released in handbook form in August, 1993.)

I have made it possible for anyone to understand and see how a diagnosis of ADD should be made. It doesn't take a college education to understand my testing process.

I feel confident that any professional who takes my training will be convinced that this is the best, most thorough, easiest, and cheapest ADD testing in the United States. I'm so confident of this that I guarantee to refund anyone's money who takes the training and doesn't feel this way.

There are very few things of which I'm so confident, but this is one of them. This testing process will never become obsolete. Yes, I said never. I may modify a few things, but the basics will never change. To explain further, I will use the analogy of headaches. For eternity, a headache has always had the same symptoms. Cave men, the prophets, kings and queens, the disciples, presidents, and dictators have had the <u>exact</u> same headache symptoms. This has never changed!

I'm sure the <u>cause</u> and treatment methods for a headache were argued, but the <u>symptoms</u> remained the same. This is the case with ADD. The cause and treatment of ADD will be argued forever, but the symptoms will remain the same.

This is what my evaluation process measures. It measures the symptoms of ADD that will <u>always</u> be present, regardless of the new discoveries in research on the brain, genetics or any other area. New discoveries may <u>add to</u> my evaluation process, but they will never replace it. Even if research discovers the actual "<u>gene</u>" that causes ADD, the symptoms will still be the same. These will not automatically disappear just because someone writes an article or book.

If a person has ADD, they will have symptoms that can be accurately measured by my evaluation process.

In addition to the actual tests administered, other factors are important to insuring a correct diagnosis.

Because ADD exists from an early age, it is necessary to obtain information about an adult's childhood. Therefore, the following information is geared toward children.

First, it must be emphasized that the evaluation of ADD children is difficult. This means that the evaluation of teenagers and adults is even more complicated. This is primarily due to the fact that the older a person gets, other events occur that masks ADD. Since school is no longer a large part of an adult's life, academic problems are not a reliable measure.

ADD consists of more than academic problems, but this is the easiest way to identify it. Academic problems can be easily measured and observed. As an ADD person gets older, they may have developed coping techniques that allow them to "mask" academic problems.

This means that the testing used for children may not be as useful when testing adults.

However, it is possible to test people for ADD, regardless of their age. Obviously, different methods have to be used. There's no one psychological test, blood test, neurological test, or achievement test that will tell you whether or not a person has ADD. The most important factor in testing and diagnosing a person correctly is having someone who is experienced in dealing with this disorder. Do not assume that all professionals know how to properly test for ADD, especially in adults.

The information I'm presenting here will probably put you ahead of most professionals, in terms of their knowledge about ADD. This is especially the case in diagnosing it. A professional must ask the right questions. The professional needs a great deal of background information in order to understand how this person functioned from the time they were in the first grade.

I'm saying that you must trust your judgement and challenge your professional. After you learn more about ADD, you will be able to ask intelligent questions. If the professional cannot answer a question to your satisfaction, I would suggest that you go to another.

Pediatricians and Psychiatrists make mistakes just like anyone, therefore, do not be impressed merely by the credentials of a professional. The information in this book will not totally enable you to diagnose someone with ADD, but you will have more information at your fingertips than many professionals. Therefore, I suggest you go to a professional and be prepared to ask him questions. This will force him to expose his knowledge, or lack of knowledge, of ADD.

This Evaluation Section is to be used as a guideline. You must remember that personal judgement and personal contact with a person cannot be duplicated in a book.

WHO CAN DO THE TESTING?

Psychiatrists and Medical Doctors are not qualified to test for ADD.

They are the only ones qualified to provide the treatment (i.e. medication), but the actual testing is out of their area of expertise.

Here is why: ADD is a physiological problem but the symptoms manifest themselves through academic, behavioral or emotional problems. Some of the symptoms of which I speak are distractibility, trouble concentrating, strong emotional reactions and poor comprehension.

The tests used to measure these areas are not medical tests. The tests used are performance, academic, or personality tests. Doctors have no experience with these tests.

Psychologists and diagnosticians are not qualified to test for ADD.

Although they have the training to administer the proper tests, they are not trained on how to administer them for ADD. In other words, the colleges that teach them how to do testing, teach them how to administer tests in a specific way. They are not allowed to deviate from this method. This method is appropriate when testing a person's I.Q. or academic abilities. It is not adequate when testing for ADD. Therefore, the results they get will not be valid for determining the presence or absence of ADD.

The "traditional" testing methods will only "pick up" or identify the person who has all the classic symptoms of ADD. If a person has all the classic symptoms, testing is nothing more than a formality. It doesn't take much training to identify an ADD person with classic symptoms. Unfortunately, most people with ADD do not have all of the classic symptoms. This is why so many are overlooked. This is why I developed an evaluation process.

Most professionals know that they don't know how to test for ADD. This doesn't stop them from doing it anyway.

The most common "testing" methods they use are superficial and simplistic.

Professionals often use questionnaires to "test" for ADD. These are inadequate and incomplete. They should be used, but they are only a small part of the testing process. The reason professionals use these questionnaires is because they don't know what else to do.

Many professionals develop questionnaires and long forms for parents to complete. They do this in order to kill time and make it appear that they are "<u>earning</u>" their money. Since the parents are billed $300 - $500 for the testing, the professional recognizes that he must make the parents "<u>feel</u>" that they got their money's worth. They do this by making the parents suffer. They try to give the impression that they are really working, analyzing, and using some "<u>mystical</u>" abilities in determining whether or not the child has ADD. In reality, these professionals often make a decision after reading the questionnaire. This takes about 3 minutes.

One of the reasons professionals don't do ADD testing on adults is because they can't "<u>bluff</u>" them. Adults are involved in the process from the beginning. When testing children, the professional and child are alone. The parents have to rely on the examiner. The examiner has control, and a child is not going to challenge the adult.

When an adult is being tested, they know what is going on. Even if they have ADD, they are smart enough to recognize a "con job". They may confront the professional and ask him to explain the rationale for certain tests. This is where the professional gets stumped, because he may not have a rationale. Professionals are not accustomed to explaining themselves, therefore, they avoid testing adults.

As you can see, the testing for ADD requires a special combination of skills and knowledge that very few people have. This is why it has never been established as to which group of professionals have "jurisdiction" over ADD. ADD actually falls between the field of medicine, psychology and education.

Many professionals are taking unfair advantage of the confusion surrounding the evaluation process. Some have good intentions, but they don't know what tests to administer or what to look for in the results. Hopefully, I can reduce the confusion surrounding the evaluation process by training others in the methods I have developed over the past few years.

It's extremely important that the testing for ADD be consistent throughout the United States. If this isn't done, ADD will continue to be overlooked and mistreated.

Training in the Testing Methods

To properly test for ADD requires a combination of skills. Therefore, I only teach the evaluation techniques in person. I've discovered that this is one aspect of ADD that I cannot teach through a book.

It takes several days of training to learn these techniques. If you are interested in the training, contact me at Forresst Publishing. It doesn't matter if you are a professional or not, you can still take the training. You won't be able to go out and do testing because you need certain credentials to obtain some of the test materials. However, you could learn a great deal about ADD.

CHAPTER 14

AUTHOR'S LETTER TO INDIVIDUAL FAMILY MEMBERS

To the ADD Adult:

Everything in your life has been affected by your ADD. Your job, your relationships, your emotions, the clothing you choose, the friends you choose, and the music you like. I can't explain the mechanism involved, and exactly <u>how</u> it affected these areas. No one can.

However, some were greatly affected by ADD, others were affected little. All I can tell you is that everything in your life was affected to <u>some</u> degree. Some were important and some were not. Some were negative and some were positive.

Unfortunately, the negatives probably out- weighed the positive. I hope to help you understand some of these negative experiences.

You are not crazy or stupid, even though you have thought you were at some point in time. You may have even considered suicide because you felt as if you didn't "fit in". After reading my book, you may now have an understanding of why you didn't fit in.

You have probably felt that no one understood you. You were right. They may still mis-understand you or not believe you have ADD. You have probably "turned over a new leaf" several times in your life but were unable to sustain your commitment. You have criticized yourself more than others have, but no one would believe it because of your "attitude".

You were probably difficult to deal with as a child. Your parents didn't know you had ADD. This isn't their fault. They did the best they could with what they had. If someone had told them about ADD and how to properly treat it, your life might have been different. The relationship between you and your parents may have been different also. Don't blame your parent for your current situation. If you want to blame anything, blame the lack of knowledge about ADD among society.

Blaming parents makes no sense anyway. If we blame parents, then the parents can blame their parents, and their parents can blame their parents. It would never end. You have to start with yourself and go from here.

Please take note of my next statement. <u>You will always be held responsible for your behavior</u>.

<u>Technically</u>, some of your behavior is <u>not</u> under your control. <u>Legally</u>, <u>all</u> of your behavior <u>is</u> your fault. Please look at these two words: <u>Technically</u> and <u>Legally</u>. I emphasize these words because people continually confuse them.

<u>Technically</u>, ADD is a chemical imbalance that you can't control. This chemical imbalance contributes to your choice of behavior.

Legally, your behavior will be blamed on you. This only makes sense. Who else can be blamed?

Having ADD will not excuse you from suffering the consequences of your actions. This is why it's extremely important that you receive the proper treatment (medication).

You may not like the idea of taking medication. To save time, I'll list some of the common statements you've made:

1. "I like the way I am. I don't want to change my personality."

   Response: Truthfully, you've never seen your true personality. Since birth, you've had a chemical imbalance. I'm sorry, but the reality is, you were born with a physical problem that makes it almost impossible for you to function like others. This isn't bad ... this isn't good ... it's just reality.

When you treat your physical problem, then you will be able to develop your real personality.

When treated, your positive traits will remain or be enhanced, and your negative traits will be modified. You will gain much more than you lose.

2. "God made me like this, so he must have had a purpose. Therefore, I shouldn't change what he/she did."

Response: I don't want to get into a long
              discussion about religion and God.
              However, the best response I can give
              you is one that I saw in a movie called
              "Oh God", with George Burns. Here is
              the dialogue (Not exactly the same
              words used, but close):

              Q: God, why do you allow bad
                    things to happen?
              God: I don't allow them to happen,
                    they just happen. I can't do
                    anything about it.
              Q: But you're God. What do you
                    mean, you can't do anything?
              God: It's built into the system. For
                    example; have you ever seen an
                    up without a down, a front
                    without a back, a top without a
                    bottom? One can't exist without
                    the other. It's the same with
                    good and bad. You can't have
                    good without having bad. It's
                    just built into the system.

I'll not try to challenge any of your religious
beliefs, regardless of what they are. Therefore, I
will challenge your statement on the basis of logic.

Your basic premise is, that we should not change
anything about ourselves ... Do I have to go any
further? Unless you are totally unreasonable, you
will have to admit that this doesn't make any sense.

3. "I'm afraid of becoming addicted to drugs."

Response: Research shows that this doesn't happen. As a matter of fact, ADD adults are more likely to abuse drugs or alcohol if not treated with medication. They may treat themselves with other drugs and this can be dangerous.

To the non-ADD siblings:

If your ADD sibling had been properly treated for ADD as a child, there is a good chance that your relationship would have been different (possibly better). Therefore, instead of looking for psychological explanations for his or her behavior, think about ADD as an explanation instead. This will be hard to do because you probably have some negative feelings about your sibling that may be hard to overcome. You may not want to find an explanation for their behavior because you've already made up your mind as to the cause. Re-thinking your decision might cause you some emotional turmoil that you would rather avoid. I understand, but please remember that life is short. In 100 years, who is going to know, or care, about the specific hard feelings you had toward your sibling? The answer is, no-one. Maintaining a negative emotion is a waste of energy, especially if it's based upon a false assumption. For your sake, let it go.

To the Child of an ADD Parent:

It doesn't matter if you have ADD or not, if your parent had ADD, they were probably much different than the average parent.

They probably over-reacted or under-reacted to your successes or failures. They may have been overly emotional or more reserved than other parents. As a matter of fact, they probably fluctuated between being the warmest and kindest person in the world, to being the coldest and most domineering. All of this was confusing to you as a child, and perhaps even now.

What I want to tell you is that this erratic behavior had very little to do with you. They may claim it did, because you were <u>there</u>. Since they never knew they had ADD and were never treated for it, they had no idea that their behavior was extreme. They just assumed that they were dealing with the normal stressors of being a parent. This was true, but their <u>response</u> to these stressors was not "normal".

When they told you that they would visit you or take you someplace and then didn't show up, they didn't do it on purpose. You probably thought that they didn't love you. This isn't true. They are disorganized, forgetful, impulsive and irresponsible. These are typical traits of ADD adults. They probably had the best of intentions, but were unable to carry through.

This may be of <u>no</u> consolation to you. You may not <u>care</u> that they have ADD. I understand why you feel that way. However, if they had been in a wheelchair or blind, you would have understood why they couldn't do things like other parents.

ADD is a physiological problem but it's not as easily seen as those just mentioned. It wasn't their fault they had ADD. They were born with it. Please, at least think about this.

To the Parents:

Don't blame yourself for not doing something earlier. Again, if you had heard about ADD at an earlier time, you might have been motivated to do something differently. You probably went to several professionals. Even if they mentioned ADD or medication, they may not have explained how serious it was. If they had, you may have made a decision to try the medication. The lack of knowledge of ADD among professionals and society at large is once again to blame. You were probably more conscientious than most parents because you had to work much harder, just to get your child to do the simple things in life. What you need to understand, is that very few people will ever understand, what you went through. This includes your spouse.

I would like to pin-point the mother at this time. You have received the brunt of criticism from other people, including your husband. You were probably blamed for being too rough on one day, and too lenient on another day. Others did not understand that you had to do this. You had to adapt to your ADD child's moods.

You will never know what you prevented in your childs life. The only thing that most of us think about, is what happened in our life. We never think about what didn't happen. I can almost guarantee that you prevented more negative things in your child's life than you created. Unfortunately, no one, including your child, will ever know, because we can never point at what it was you prevented.

The best example I can give is this: if you walk down Elm Street and get hit by a car; what would have happened if you had walked down Pine Street instead? We can never know because you can't do both. Who knows, if you had walked down Pine Street, you might have been hit by a <u>bus</u>.

Another example: A parent screams and yells at their ADD child who is running toward the street. The parent says and does anything possible to make the child stop. They may yell, scream, threaten or cuss the child. The child stops running toward the street, and doesn't notice the truck that just passed. He only sees what the parent <u>did</u>. He doesn't see what the parent prevented (ie: getting hit by a truck).

ADD parents are often concerned that they have emotionally damaged their ADD child. My response often surprises them because I say, you <u>probably did</u>. But, you probably <u>prevented</u> something much worse.

This emotional damage was not inflicted on purpose, but it probably did occur. "Emotional damage" usually occurs when you are harsh on a child. Unfortunately, parents often have to be extremely harsh on the ADD child, just to get them to listen to their directives.

I know of ADD children who are lucky that their parents were harsh on them. Otherwise, they would be dead. They would have been hit by a car or drowned if the parents had not put the <u>"fear of God"</u> in them. These two examples of what was <u>prevented</u> are easily seen and easily understood. Other examples of what parents prevent are not as easily seen because they involve emotional or psychological issues.

My main point is this: yes, you have damaged your child's emotional well being; however, you may have prevented something much worse than this.

If you <u>intentionally</u> damaged them, then I offer you <u>no</u> compassion. However, I've discovered that most parents of ADD children do not do so intentionally. You probably told your child that you hope they have a child just like them so they have to endure the same grief. It's very likely that this will happen. Some of your grandchildren will probably have ADD. Therefore, don't start blaming your child for the grandchildren's behavior. Show compassion and try to remember what you had to put up with.

Try to remember how no one understood what you were going through. Your child is going through the same thing and they need your help.

CHAPTER 15

LETTER TO PROFESSIONALS

Dear Professional:

If you've been working in the mental Health Field for more than five years, and haven't encountered a large number of people with ADD, then you have been incompetent.

You work with a special population of people (i.e. people with problems). This special population of people has a higher incidence of ADD individuals than the 3 to 10% in the average population. Therefore, there are a lot of ADD people in your practice, whether you know it or not. You have misdiagnosed and mistreated them. You have had few successes with counseling these people because ADD was the biggest cause of their problems and should have been your focus.

You've made a lot of money by counseling them on a weekly basis for 1 or 2 years. Yes, they tell you they feel better after talking to you but you have not yet solved their chemical imbalance. This is why they come back every week. They hope that if they talk with you enough times, that this good feeling they have will stay with them the rest of the week. It never does.

You've been responsible for ruining the lives of hundreds of people because you haven't learned enough about ADD. They may have come to you with a child having behavior problems, and your first thought was to blame the parents. Your first thought should have been ADD because it is more common. You may have counseled this family for a year or two before they dropped out. What you haven't seen is what happened to that individual 5, 10, or 15 years later.

Because you were incompetent and overlooked their ADD, some are now in prison, alcoholic/drug users, or dead.

This may not have happened if you had diagnosed them as having ADD.

The aforementioned part of this letter is extremely negative. I'm sorry, but someone needed to tell you how your incompetence about ADD has harmed the people you wanted to help.

I hope that from this negative letter, something positive will occur. I hope that from this point forward you pay more attention to ADD. It's too late for the people whose lives you ruined in the past 5 or more years. However, it's not too late for the people who come to see you now.

Don't be stubborn and refuse to admit (to yourself) that you've been incompetent for all these years. Just accept it and change. If you remain stubborn, you will continue to ruin people's lives.

Here is how I changed my thinking about people who came into my office for counseling, especially when they sought help for their child. I hope this helps you change your thinking.

Ask yourself this question:

Do <u>Bad</u> parents voluntarily come to therapists and spend thousands of dollars in finding help for their child?

The answer is <u>No</u>! These are signs of good conscientious parents.

Therefore, why would you automatically think the parents are to blame for their child's problems? I know that you do this. I did, until I studied ADD.

You, just like the parents, are searching for an explanation as to why this child does what he does. Since you don't understand ADD, your first inclination is to blame the parents or at least be suspicious of the parents. You may think they are nice people but in the back of your mind you may think there is a <u>dark</u> side that is causing this child to have problems. Again, what other explanation could there be?

When you get to this point, go back to my original question. Do <u>Bad</u> parents seek the services of someone like you? No they don't! Therefore, <u>listen</u> to what the parents have to say and think about ADD. Don't be stubborn. Swallow your pride and accept the fact that you missed it for a few weeks or months. The parents will understand and will be extremely happy that someone finally found the problem. When it comes to their children, parents don't mind spending their money,

<u>if</u> it's going to help. They don't like spending their money and receiving nothing in return. I don't blame them.

Don't worry about other professionals accusing you of over-diagnosing ADD.

They don't understand ADD and will try to justify their continued ignorance of this disorder.

Don't worry about schools or other professionals reducing their referrals to you because of your work with ADD. You will receive the majority of your referrals from word of mouth. Because you get <u>results</u> from treating children, parents will spread the word.

Once you start diagnosing and <u>properly</u> treating ADD (ie: with medication), you will receive the personal satisfaction of knowing that you have significantly changed someone's life. The reason you will know it is because you will <u>see it</u>. You will see it within <u>weeks</u>, not years. You will then be confident that what I've been telling you is true.

Good Luck,

Glenn Hunsucker

<u>Diplomatic</u> Letter to Doctors

The following letter is for those who encounter a resistant doctor. I've discovered that if you approach them <u>properly</u>, they may be willing to cooperate. Here is an example of how to approach them. You can use this letter or, you can use this information in a face to face meeting with the doctor.

To Attending Physician:

I recently read a book on ADD by Glenn Hunsucker that closely resembles symptoms and experiences my child had (I had) all his life.

I am not a hypochondriac and do not jump to conclusions when a new disease or disorder appears on the scene. Therefore, please don't assume that I have not thoroughly thought about the information in this letter.

We have been to several doctors, psychologists, and have had numerous consultations with school personnel, but they have not been able to help us. We have spent a great deal of money on counseling, both individual and family. It has helped some areas but did not solve the problem for which we initially sought help.

No one has ever been able to give a logical explanation until I read Mr. Hunsucker's book. He not only explains why my child (I) has academic and behavior problems, but he also explains why so many professionals have been unable to help us.

It may be difficult for you to believe that a book could give a lay-person such as myself enough information for me to be so confident that ADD is the problem. However, Mr. Hunsucker specifically points out that this is <u>exactly</u> why he wrote the book as he did.

He recognized that for a variety of reasons, most professionals overlook ADD (especially in adults). Therefore, he chose to write a book that gives the lay-person enough information to recognize symptoms that professionals never see because they don't live with the child (me). In essence, his book gives the average person the ability to make a decision on the presence or absence of ADD by using the "mathematics of probability".

Based on all that I have read, ADD has a higher probability of being the problem than anything else. There are just too many similarities between his book and my child's (my) life for it to be mere coincidence.

This letter is to ask for your help in treating my child (me) with medication. Personally, I don't like the idea of my child (me) being on medication. However, Mr. Hunsucker points out that ADD is a chemical imbalance and the only treatment proven to be effective is medication. Therefore, I'm willing to try the medication for the benefit of my child (me).

If you feel uncomfortable prescribing the medication, I would be glad to talk with you further or let you read Mr. Hunsucker's book. I would like to suggest an alternate plan that would involve a limited trial period of the medication.

If we could just try the medication for four to six weeks, with periodic visits to your office during this time, a definite decision as to the benefits, or lack of same, could be made.

The medication may not help, but I would be re-miss if I didn't at least try it for a short period of time. The emotional pain and suffering my child (I) endures is the reason I'm making this request.

If the medication helps him (me), I will be forever grateful. If it doesn't, then at least we tried and I will no longer wonder if this was the answer.

Thank you for your time, and please feel free to contact me at any time.

Letter To Those Who Don't Believe ADD Exists

Dear Cynic:

It's unlikely that I can change what you believe. So, we must first discuss the difference between <u>belief</u> and <u>knowledge</u>. The best way to avoid a long boring explanation is to provide an example.

There are people, <u>today</u>, who <u>believe</u> that the world is <u>flat</u> (Flat Earth Society).

Very simply, they are either right, or they are wrong.

The majority of people on earth <u>know</u> that the world is round (oblong). This view was influenced by the overwhelming amount of evidence that increased their <u>knowledge</u>.

Those in the Flat Earth Society always have an alternative explanation. Their stance can be summarized by the phrase, "Don't confuse me with the facts".

Now, in conjunction with ADD, there is a big difference between <u>believing</u> ADD exists and <u>knowing</u> it exists.

You don't <u>believe</u> it exists and I <u>know</u> it exists.

The only reason you don't believe ADD exists is because you don't want to put out the effort to gain knowledge. Gaining knowledge is hard because it may make you re-think your views.

"Ignorance Is Bliss"

I think that if you researched ADD, you would become one of the staunchest supporters of ADD. I've seen this happen quite often. I've had fathers who didn't believe that anything was wrong with their sons and that coming to see me was stupid. They didn't believe in ADD or the medication.

Once their child was treated, they changed their minds and became some of my best advocates. They saw how their child had improved both academically and emotionally.

In closing, I understand why you don't believe ADD exists. You lack knowledge about ADD.

This is O.K. I don't expect everyone to get deeply involved with ADD. All I ask is that you don't voice your <u>beliefs</u> in such a way that suggests that your views are based on <u>knowledge</u>.

Sincerely, Glenn Hunsucker

P.S. If you think about some of the things that you believe, I think you will find that many of them are more difficult to believe than a chemical imbalance (ADD).

Psychological principals such as multiple personalities are more difficult to believe than a chemical imbalance. Believing in Einstein's theories or that of other scientists, is harder to believe than ADD. Even believing in God is more theoretical than ADD. ADD, a chemical imbalance, is simple in comparison to the aforementioned.

CHAPTER 16

FUTURE OF ADD

This is the 2nd Book I've written on ADD. This year (1993), I will try to finish 4 more (I have 7 books I want to write). To accomplish this, I've reduced my practice to the point that I will do <u>nothing</u> but write for several months (maybe years).

The reason I'm telling you this is to let you know that there is more information about ADD yet to come. It seems that every large publisher in the U.S. has realized that my books sell. Several have spoken with me and asked the same question: Why does your book sell better than others? They never believe my answer, so they assume that the topic, ADD, is the reason. Consequently they hurriedly publish an ADD book with a famous name attached, hoping to capitalize on the "market."

They are then surprised when their books don't sell as well as mine. They don't understand that I work and write about nothing but ADD. I have a deep interest and understanding of this disorder. I don't write <u>just</u> to <u>sell</u> books. I write to communicate information on ADD. I also publish my own books which means I can write the way I choose.

These multi-million dollar publishers are only interested in _selling_ books. ADD is only _one_ topic of the thousands with which they work. Consequently their books on ADD are often superficial and _"packaged."_

For those of you who don't know about large book publishers, the _"Author"_ doesn't have control over what he writes. These large publishers have a staff that "edits" the information to be presented. This means that the person who has control over the information to be presented in an ADD book, is a person who knows very _little_ or absolutely _nothing_, about ADD. They know sentence structure, proper grammar, synonyms, and how to protect their employer. Because these publishers have thousands of books on different topics, editors of ADD books have to omit statements that could be offensive to _any_ potential customer. Therefore, they use "safe" words that are bland or vague. This leads to the superficial and "packaged" ADD books to which I previously referred. The editor basically "writes" the book, while the author is merely used for his credentials or popularity. This is done to improve the _marketing_ of the _product_ (ADD).

In other words, give these large publishers a topic that is _selling_ and they will have a book on it by _next week_. Don't get me wrong, this is the free enterprise system and I understand business. However, ADD is an extremely serious disorder that has ruined the lives of thousands of people. When large publishing companies, with millions of dollars, _flood_ the market with these superficial books on ADD, thousands of people are _harmed_.

To be fair, these large companies have no idea how much harm they are doing. They don't understand ADD, so they think that any and all books on ADD are the same. They are wrong.

Several large publishers have <u>called me</u>, because they felt that they might want to publish my first book. After reviewing it, they decided that my statements were too controversial for them to publish. Ironically, they admit that my book has sold more copies than any other ADD book. They say that they don't understand why, because it's <u>badly</u> written, I'm not a medical doctor, the type style is "odd", it's self-published, and the cover is <u>not</u> appealing ... aside from being <u>rude</u>, this shows just how much <u>"out of touch"</u> with the average person these publishers have become. The average person is interested in <u>good information</u>, not superficiality. When they find it, they overlook the cosmetic, and listen to the message. I write my books with this in mind.

In compiling the information for my books, I try to read all the ADD research available. In addition to this, I read the research in areas that are only vaguely related to ADD. These areas often provide new insight or ideas. I also rely on my professional experience with hundreds of adults and children. The one other ingredient I include in my books that the large publishing companies seem to dislike and avoid, is <u>common sense</u>.

By common sense I only mean that I explain how and why, I make certain statements or come to certain conclusions. I want the reader to decide, on their own, as to whether or not I make sense.

I <u>don't</u> write for professionals or researchers. I write for the average person. I <u>don't</u> view the reader as someone <u>beneath</u> me. Therefore, I feel that I owe them an explanation as to why I make certain statements, or come to certain conclusions. Too often, publishers and authors on ADD seem to view the reader as a <u>blank slate</u>. In other words, they merely list facts or information and expect the reader to accept it, without question. (personally, I feel that this is a big problem in our society. We don't encourage people to <u>think</u> for themselves.) This is how <u>false</u> information on ADD becomes accepted as true. Especially if its repeated year after year.

Because of the aforementioned, my perspective and approach to writing books on ADD is much different than others. Other books maintain a narrow focus and they seem to assume that research will solve the ADD problem. Therefore, they <u>rigidly</u> report the research findings. They don't use their analytical thinking abilities to predict how these findings could effect the future.

I go beyond the mere reporting of facts. I give my views of the significance of these findings to our future. Researchers and professionals dislike this because it is <u>"unscientific"</u>.

My response to this is best summarized by the following phrase:

"All great discoveries were ideas first." Thousands of years ago, there were people who used their <u>thinking abilities</u> to determine that the Earth revolved around the Sun. This was a dangerous view to hold because it challenged the views of the "scientists" and religious leaders. The earth was seen as the <u>center</u> of the universe and everything revolved around it. These "ideas" were ignored for years because they were not

<u>scientifically</u> proven. Needless to say, science finally caught up with good analytical thinking and discovered that these "unscientific" ideas were correct.

This is only one example of the thousands of ideas and theories that have been ignored because of the lack of scientific evidence. This situation continues today. I just happen to be one of the people involved in this age-old problem because of my views on ADD. As stated in other parts of this book, the kind of research needed on ADD can't be done.

Because of this, there are only two options. One is to do the research, report it, and do nothing. The other is to analyze the findings and make predictions as to how our future could be effected. From this, we can then develop a plan of action to <u>prevent</u> future problems. This second option requires an element of risk.

I have chosen the second option. I recognize that this approach opens me to criticism from professionals and the scientific community. But, as in all decisions, there are positives and negatives. In my estimation, the negative criticism I receive is small, in contrast to the positive impact I can have in the lives of others.

Therefore I am going to make a prediction. I predict that the crime rate (especially among teens), alcohol/drug use, the drop-out rate and the number of irresponsible workers will increase. In ten years, (this is 1993). I feel these will be much worse than they are today. (<u>Unless</u>... unless ADD is dealt with properly.)

Am I crazy? Maybe so.

However, I <u>know</u> that ADD is not being recognized or treated properly. It's unlikely that this will change in the next ten years.

Consider this: It is a <u>fact</u> that the number of people with ADD increases <u>every day</u>. Why? Because it's <u>hereditary</u>. This means that the problems caused by ADD will increase. (ie: crime, alcohol/drug abuse, dropouts, irresponsible workers.) The <u>problems</u> will not increase immediately. It will take ten years or more for the accumulative effect to be noticed.

I hope this book contributes to turning things around.

I want to at least <u>document</u> the fact that ADD was predicted to be a serious problem for our society. I <u>hope</u> I'm wrong.

I am sick and tired of hearing professionals say that information on ADD is new. It is <u>not</u> new. This statement is another cover up by the professional community.

If we do not start diagnosing and treating ADD at an early age, I see it as having one of the biggest negative impacts on our society since Aids. It may be more serious than Aids because, unlike Aids, treatment isn't the problem. We have the treatment. Getting it recognized by society is the problem. Getting it <u>properly</u> diagnosed and treated by the professionals is the biggest problem.

The number of people with ADD is slowly increasing. Because the increase is gradual, it is difficult to see how these untreated ADD individuals are changing the <u>values</u> of our society, but they are.

Consider this: the values of 100,000 untreated ADD adults will have a different impact on society than 200,000 untreated ADD adults. As time marches on and the numbers of untreated ADD adults increase, their views and morals will become more accepted as the norm. At the present time, only about 10% of the population has ADD. In 30 or 40 years, it may be as high as 30%. This many people with ADD will definitely have an impact on society. They will have a big impact on a city, if a large number of them gravitate to the same area.

I see this occurring at the present time. Many people with ADD are creative and talented, especially in music and acting. They are attractive, charismatic, and intelligent. They gravitate towards professions that give them media exposure.

Needless to say, the people who have the opportunity to influence our society are those who become famous as singers or movie stars. These people gain influence because of their position and money. Because of media exposure, their personal views on a number of topics are often presented at length. There is no doubt that their views influence others, even if these views are somewhat bizarre. (Unfortunately, the majority of ADD adults do not have views that are beneficial to society. Those who do, are outnumbered by a large margin.)

ADD youngsters are already causing the biggest problems in the educational system (ie: dropouts and slow learners). ADD teens account for a large percentage of juvenile crime. What will happen in ten years if this group continues to increase? We don't know, but the results are probably more negative than positive.

I recognize that there will <u>always</u> be some <u>degree</u> of alcohol/drug abuse, crime, dropouts, and irresponsible workers in society. These have <u>nothing</u> to do with ADD. These will remain at a fairly constant level from year to year.

However, I'm saying that ADD is increasing the <u>degree</u> or number of these problems, because the number of people with ADD is <u>not</u> remaining constant. It is increasing.

There is a Solution

What I'm going to say next may sound <u>strange</u>, idealistic, or absurd. I say these problems can be solved <u>easily, cheaply, and quickly</u>.

Who would believe me if I said I could save the tax payers billions of dollars per year and at the same time decrease alcohol/drug abuse, crime, and increase academic test scores? What if I also said, I could do it for less than 5 million dollars and the results would be <u>observable</u> in one year (maybe less)? (I'm already having an impact and I don't have anything close to 5 million). Note: I said <u>5 million dollars</u>. I didn't say <u>per year</u>; I didn't say per <u>state</u>. I said 5 million dollars, for 20 years, for the entire United States. To go even further, I would give a <u>money back guarantee</u>. If the results weren't observable and significant (within a specified time) I would refund the entire 5 million dollars. Yes, the money would still be available.

I will go even one step further: <u>Loan</u> me 5 million dollars and I will still do it. It won't cost the tax payer a thing. I know this sounds ridiculous to many people. Especially to those who have been working on these problems for years and have spent billions of our tax dollars on useless programs.

They <u>hope</u> I'm wrong. They wouldn't want me to succeed because this would prove them wrong. Their competence would be questioned. They want these problems to appear <u>unsolvable</u>. I'm absolutely positively convinced that these problems can be solved cheaply and quickly. (I've done it on a <u>small</u> scale because of my <u>small</u> bank roll.)

These are <u>not mystical</u> problems! Pollution and the deterioration of the ozone layer are problems that are hard to solve because they are irreversible.

Crime, alcohol/drug abuse, incompetent workers, and low academic achievement scores are problems that <u>can</u> be reversed.

REFERENCES

Abrahamsen, D. Confessions of Son of Sam. New York: Columbia University Press, 1985.

Alberts-Corush, Jody: Firestone, Phillip: and Goodman, John T. Attention and Impulsivity Characteristics of the Biological and Adoptive Parents of Hyperactive and Normal Control Children. American Journal of Orthopsychiatry, Vol. 56 (3), 413-423, July 1986.

Amado, H., and Lustman, P. Attention Deficit Disorders in Three Young Adults. Journal of Psychiatric Treatment and Evaluation, Vol. 5, 121-125, 1983.

American Psychiatric Association DSM III-R, Washington D.C., 1987.

Barkley, R. A. A review of Stimulant Drug Research with Hyperactive Children. Journal of Child Psychology and Psychiatry, 18, 137-165, 1977.

Barkley, R. A. Hyperactive Children, New York: Guilford Press, 1981.

Bassuk, Ellen L. The Practitioners Guide to Psychoactive Drugs (2nd Ed). New York: Plenum Medical Book Company, 1983.

Bell, R. Q. Socialization Findings Re-examined. In R. Q. Bell and L. Harper (EDS.), Child Effects on Adults. New York: Wiley, 1977.

Biederman, J. and Steingard, R. Attention-Deficit Hyperactivity Disorder in Adolescents. Psychiatric Annuls, Vol. 19 (11), 587-596, 1989.

Bloomingdale, Lewis B. W. A.D.D. Psychiatric Journal of the University of Ottowa, Vol. 9 (4), Dec. 1984.

Borden, K. A.: Brown, R.T.: and Clingerman, S. R. Validity of Attention Deficit Disorder; A Second Look. American Journal of Orthopsychiatry, Vol. 55 (3), 466-467, 1985.

Borland, B. L., and Heckman, H. K. Hyperactive Boys and their Brothers: A 25-Year Follow-up Study. Archives of General Psychiatry, 33, 669-675, 1976.

Brown, D.: Winsberg, B.: Bialer, I.: et al. Imipramine Therapy and Seizures. Three Children Treated for Hyperactive Behavior Disorders. AM J Psychiatry, 130, 210-212, 1972.

Bryant, Ernest T.: Scott, Monte L.: Golden, Charles J.: and Tori, Christopher D. Neuropsychological Deficits, Learning Disability, and Violent Behavior. Vol. 52 (2), 323-324, 1984.

Cantwell, D.P. The Attention Deficit Disorder Syndrome, Current Knowledge, Future Needs. Journal of the American Academy of Child Psychiatry, Vol.23 (3), 315-318, May 1984.

Cantwell, D. P. Psychiatric Illness in the Families of Hyperactive Children. Archives of General Psychiatry, 27, 414-427, 1972.

Caparulo, B. K.: Cohen, D. J.: Rothman, S. L.: Young, J.G.: Katz, J.D.: Shaywitz, S.E.: and Shaywitz, B.A. Computed Tomographic Brain Scanning in Children with Developmental Neuropsychiatric Disorders. Annual Progress in Child Psychiatry and Child Development. New York: Brunner/Mazel, 1982.

Carlson, Gabrielle A., and Rapport, Mark D. Diagnostic Classification Issues in Attention - Deficit Hyperactivity Disorder. Psychiatric Annuls, Vol. 19, (11), 576-583, 1989.

Clampit, M. K., and Pickle, J. B. Stimulant Medication and the Hyperactive Adolescent: Myths and Facts. Adolescence, Vol. 18 (72), 812-822, Winter 1983.

Conners, C. K. Food Additives and Hyperactive Children. New York: Plenum, 1980.

Feldman, S.: Denhoff, E.: And Denhoff, J. The Attention Disorders and Related Syndromes: Outcome in Adolescence & Young Adult Life. In E. Denhoff and L. Stern (EDS.), Minimal Brain Dysfunction: A Developmental Approach. New York: Masson Publishing (USA), 1979.

Fleisher, L. S.: Soodak, L. C.: and Jelin, M. A. Selective Attention Deficits in Learning Disabled Children: Analysis of the Data Base. Exceptional Children, Vol. 51, No. 2, 136-141, Oct. 1984.

Gillberg, C. I., and Gillberg, C. Three Year Follow-up at age 10 as Children with Minor Neurodevelopmental Disorders I: Behavioral Problems. Developmental Medicine and Child Neurology, Vol. 25 (4), 438-449, Aug. 1983.

Gittleman, R.: Mannuzza, S.: Shenker, R.: and Bonagura, N. Hyperactive Boys Almost Grown Up: Psychiatric Status. Archives of General Psychiatry.

Gomez, R. L.: Janowsky, D.: Zeitin, M.: Huey, L.: and Clopton, P. L. Adult Psychiatric Diagnosis and Symptoms Compatible with the Hyperactive Child Syndrome: A Retrospective Study. Journal of Clinical Psychiatry, 42, 389-394, 1981.

Goodwin, S. W.: Schulsinger, D.: Hermansen, L.: Guze, S. B.: and Winokur, G. Alcoholism and the Hyperactive Child Syndrome. Journal of Nervous and Mental Disease, 160, 349-353, 1975.

Goyete, C. H.: Conners, C. K.: and Ulrich, R. F. Normative Data on Revised Conners Parent and Teacher Rating Scales. Journal of Abnormal Child Psychology, 6, 221-236, 1978.

Gross, M. D. Growth of Hyperkinetic Children Taking Methylphenidate, Dextroamphetamine, or Imipramine/ Desipramine. Pediatrics, 58, 423-431, 1976.

Harley, J. P.: Mathews, C. G.: and Eichman, P. L. Synthetic Food Colors and Hyperactivity in Children: A Double-blind Challenge Experiment. Pediatrics, 62, 975-983, 1978.

Hechtman, Lily. Attention-Deficit Hyperactivity Disorder in Adolescence and Adulthood: An Updated Follow-up. Psychiatric Annuls, Vol. 19 (11), 597-603, 1989.

Hechtman, L., and Weiss, G. Controlled Prospective 15 Year Follow-up of Hyperactives as Adults: Non-Medical Drug and Alcohol Use and Anti - Social Behavior.

Hechtman, L.: Weiss, G.: and Perlman, T. Hyperactives as Young Adults: Self-Esteem and Social Skills. Canadian Journal of Psychiatry, 25, 478-483, 1980.

Hechtman, L.: Weiss, G.: and Perlman, T. Hyperactives as Young Adults: Past and Current Substance Abuse and Anti - Social Behavior. American Journal of Orthopsychiatry, Vol. 54 (3), 415-425, 1984.

Hechtman, L.: Wiess, G.: Perlman, T.: and Tuck, D. Hyperactives As Young Adults: Various Clinical Outcomes. Adolescent Psychiatry, 9, 295-306, 1981.

Hechtman, L.: Weiss, G.: and Perlman, T. Young Adults Outcomes of Hyperactive Children who Received Long-Term Stimulant Treatment. Journal of the American Academy of Child Psychiatry, 23, 261-270, 1984.

Hollander, H. E., and Turner, F.D. Characteristics of Incarcerated Delinquents, Relationships Between Development Disorders, Environmental and Family Factors, and Patterns of Offense and Recidivism. Journal of the American Academy of Child Psychiatry, Vol. 24 (2), 221-226, 1985.

Horn, W. F.: Chatoor, I.: and Conners, K.C. Addictive Affects of Dexedrene and Self-Control Training. Behavior Modification, Vol. 7 (3), 383-402, 1983.

Hussey, Hans R., and Howell, David C. Relationships Between Adult Alcoholism and Childhood Behavior Disorders. Psychiatric Journal of the University of Ottawa, Vol. 10 (2), 114-119, June 1985.

188

Klee, S. H.: Garfinkel, B. D.: and Beauchesne, H. Attention Deficits in Adults. Psychiatric Annuls, Vol. 16 (1), 52-56, 1986.

Kramer, John R. What are Hyperactive Children like as Young Adults? Journal of Children in Contemporary Society, Vol. 19 (1-2), 890-898, 1986.

Loney, J.: Whaley-Klahn, M. A.: Kosier, T.: and Conboy, J. Hyperactive Boys & their Brothers at 21: Predictors of Aggressive & Anti-social Outcomes. Paper presented at meeting of the Society for Life History Research, Monterey, CA, Nov. 1981

Loney, J.: Kramer, J.: and Milich, R. The Hyperkinetic Child Grows Up: Predictors of Symptoms, Delinquency, and Achievement at Follow-up. In K.D. Gadow and J. Loney, (EDS.), Psychosocial Aspects of Drug Treatment for Hyperactivity. Boulder, Colorado: Westview press, 1981.

Lufi, D., and Cohen, A. Using the WISC-R to Identify Attentional Deficit Disorder. Psychology in the Schools, Vol. 22 (1), 40-42, 1985.

Mann, H. B., and Greenspan, S. I. The Identification and Treatment of Adult Brain Dysfunction. American Journal of Psychiatry, Vol. 133, 1013-1017, 1976.

Menkes, M. M.: Rowe, J. S.: and Menkes, J. H. A Twenty-Five Year Follow-up Study on the Hyperkinetic Child with Minimal Brain Dysfunction. Pediatrics, Vol. 39 (3), 393-399, 1967.

Morrison, J. R. Childhood Hyperactivity in an Adult Psychiatric Population: Social Factors. Journal of Clinical Psychiatry, Vol. 41, 40-43, 1980.

Morrison, James R. Diagnosis of Adult Psychiatric Patients with Childhood Hyperactivity. American Journal of Psychiatry, Vol. 136, 955-958, 1979.

Morrison, J. R., and Stewart, M. A. The Psychiatric Status of the Legal Families of Adopted Hyperactive Children. Archives of General Psychiatry, 28, 888-891, 1973.

Norris, Joel. Serial Killers: The Growing Menace. Doubleday, 1988.

O'leasry, K. D.: Vivian, D.: and Cornoldi, C. Assessment and Treatment of "Hyperactivity" in Italy and the United States. Journal of Clinical Child Psychology, Vol. 13 (1), 56-60, 1984.

Ownby, Raymond L. The Neuropsychology of Attention Deficit Disorders in Children. Journal of Psychiatric Treatment and Evaluation, Vol. 5, 227-236, 1983.

Pattison, Mansell. Clinical Approaches to the Alcoholic Patient. Psychosomatics, Vol. 27, (11), 762-770, Nov. 1986.

Psyche-Media Inc. The Hyperactive Client. Psychiatric Aspects of Mental Retardation Reviews, Vol. 3 (3), Mar. 1984.

Rapoport, Judith L. Antidepressants in Childhood Attention Deficit Disorder and Obsessive Compulsive Disorder. Psychosomatics, Vol.27 (11), Nov. 1986.

Reid, William H. Treatment of the DSM III Psychiatric Disorders. New York: Brunner/Mazel, 1983.

Robins, L. N. Sturdy Childhood Predictors of Adult Outcomes: Replications from Longitudinal Studies. Psychological Medicine, 8, 611-622, 1978.

Routh, Donald K. Attention Deficit Disorder: It's Relationships with Activity, Aggression, and Achievement. Advances in Developmental and Behavioral Pediatrics, Vol. 4, 125-163, 1983.

Safer, D. J., and Krager, J. M. A Survey of Medication Treatment for Hyperactives/ Inattentive Students. Jama, Vol. 260 (15), 2256-2258, 1988.

Satel, S.: Southwick, S.: and Denton, C. Use of Imipramine for Attention Deficit Disorder in a Borderline Patient. Journal of Nervous and Mental Disease, Vol. 176 (5), 305-307, 1988.

Satterfield, J. The Hyperactive Child Syndrome, A Precursor of Adult Psychopathy. In R. Hare and D. Schalling (EDS.), Psychopathic Behavior Approaches to Research, Chichester, England: Wiley, 1976.

Shaywitz., S. E., and Shaywitz, B. A. Increased Medication Use in Attention-Deficit Hyperactivity Disorder: Regressive or Appropriate? Jama, Vol. 260 (15), 2270-2272, 1988.

Sleator, E. K., and Ullman, R. K. Can the Physician Diagnose Hyperactivity in the Office? Pediatrics, 67, 13-17, 1981.

Sovner, R., and Hurley, A. D. The Hyperactive Client. Psychiatric Aspects of Mental Retardation Reviews, Vol. 3 (3), 9-12, 1984.

Stare, F. J.: Whelan, E. M.: and Sheridan, M. Diet and Hyper-Activity: Is There a Relationship? Pediatrics, 66, 521-525, 1980.

Stewart, M. A.: De Blois, C. S.: and Singer, S. Alcoholism and Hyperactivity Revisited. In M. Gallanter, (ED.), Biomedical Issues and Clinical Effects of Alcoholism (Vol. 5). New York: Grune and Stratton, 1979.

Varley, C. K. Diet and the Behavior of Children with Attention Deficit Disorder. Journal of the American Academy of Child Psychiatry, 23 (2), 182-185, 1984.

Weiss, G.: Hechtman, L.: Perlman, T.: Hopkins, J.: and Wener, A. Hyperactives as Young Adults: A Controlled Prospective Ten Year Follow-up of 75 Children. Archives of General Psychiatry, Vol. 36, 675-681, 1979.

Weiss, G.: Hechtman, L.: and Perlman, T. Hyperactives as Young Adults: School, Employer and Self-rating Scales Obtained During Ten Year Follow-up Evaluation. American Journal of Orthopsychiatry, 48, 438-445, 1978.

Weiss, G.: Hechtman, L.: Milroy, T.: and Perlman, T. Psychiatric Status of Hyperactives as Adults: A Controlled 15 Year Follow-up of 63 Hyperactive Children. Journal of the American Academy of Child Psychiatry, 24, 211-220, 1985.

Wender, E. H.: Reimherr, F. W.: and Wood, D. R. Attention Deficit Disorder ("Minimal Brain Disfunction") in Adults. Archives of General Psychiatry, Vol. 38, 449-456, 1981.

Wender, P. H.: Reimherr, F. W.: Wood, D.: and Ward, M. A Controlled Study of Methylphenidate in the Treatment of Attention Deficit Disorder, Residual Type, in Adults. American Journal of Psychiatry, Vol. 142 (5), 547-552, 1985.

Wiener, Jerry. Attention-Deficit Hyperactivity Disorder. Psychiatric Annals, Vol. 19 (11), 574-575, 1989.

Wood, D. R.: Reimherr, F. W.: Wender, P. H.: and Johnson, G. E. Diagnosis and Treatment of Minimal Brain Dysfunction in Adults. Archives of General Psychiatry, Vol. 33, 1453-1460, 1976.

About the Author

Glenn Hunsucker has become the nation's most celebrated author on ADD. His writing style is refreshingly different because it is clear and easily understood by the average person.

Mr. Hunsucker's success is due, in part, to his honest and candid questioning of the competence of those organizations and professionals who work with ADD. He has caused a turmoil within the mental health profession that will lead to dramatic improvements in the diagnosis and treatment of ADD children and adults.

Readers have recognized that his books give them the information they need to make important decisions. He has made all other ADD books obsolete. Word of mouth popularity has resulted in his books outselling all other ADD books, including those published by the largest multi-million dollar corporations in the United States.

In the next few years, Mr. Hunsucker will publish more books on ADD than any author in history. His books have become the standard by which all others are compared, and are the first to be printed in 3 different languages. This is unprecedented!

Mr. Hunsucker's influence on the field of psychology will be felt for generations to come and will extend beyond the boundaries of this hemisphere.

Those who read his books will reach the same conclusion that hundreds of thousands of others have reached:

He has become the <u>Voice</u> of ADD.

Fact Sheet on Mr. Hunsucker

1. Founder and Executive Director of the ADD Centers in the Dallas/Fort Worth metro-plex.
2. Author of several books on ADD, including the only one to become a best seller.
3. Has developed the most comprehensive ADD Evaluation Process for children and adults in the United States.
4. Presents seminars and workshops on ADD throughout the country.
5. Has received numerous awards for his work with children.
6. Received his Bachelor's Degree in Psychology from Hardin Simmons and his Master's Degree in Psychology from Abilene Christian University.
7. Hosted a weekly T.V. show on ADD.
8. Hosted a weekly radio talk show on ADD.